G.B.S. ON MUSIC

WITH A FOREWORD BY
ALEC ROBERTSON

PENGUIN BOOKS

Penguin Books Ltd, Harmondsworth, Middlesex
AUSTRALIA: Penguin Books Pty Ltd, 762 Whitehorse Road,
Mitcham, Victoria

—

London Music in 1888–9 first published by Constable 1937
Music in London 1890–94 first published by Constable 1932
This selection first published in Pelican Books 1962
and copyright © Penguin Books, 1962

—

Made and printed in Great Britain
by Hazell Watson & Viney Ltd
Aylesbury and Slough
Set in Linotype Granjon

CONTENTS

FOREWORD

In a long article on criticism in Grove's *Dictionary of Music and Musicians*, Winton Dean sets out in detail the eight qualifications he considers that the ideal music critic should possess, and reaches the conclusion that – with some reservations as to musical history and scholarship – Bernard Shaw possesses all of them in abundant measure, a conclusion which no one who knows Shaw's volumes of music criticism is likely to contest.

It is common experience that to take up one of these books with the object of dipping into it here and there means to be irresistibly led on from page to page not only by Shaw's immensely readable style, his vivid phrases, his insight and wit, but by his sovereign power of interesting the reader in artists known to us only by name and reputation, and often not at all, and in events that may have taken place over 70 years ago.

This Penguin selection gives us, complete, the long autobiographical Preface to *London Music in 1888–9*, which contains a most entertaining account of Shaw's youthful musical experience and development; the background in fact to the criticisms of 'Corno di Bassetto', reluctantly and, as he says, shamefacedly reprinted by their author. It was, by the way, in a Note dated 1936 in this book that he retracted his biased view of Brahms, whom, amongst other epithets, he had called the Leviathan Maunderer.

The entries, in this selection, about Bayreuth, where Cosima Wagner was then reigning supreme, are extraordinarily perceptive, and if directed against the dead hand of tradition they are, here as elsewhere, invariably constructive. Shaw is equally perceptive about Mozart, who was his true love amongst composers, and in writing on the Centenary of 1891 he remarks profoundly:

Nothing but the finest execution – beautiful, expressive, and intelligent – will serve; and the worst of it is, that the phrases are so perfectly clear and straightforward, that you are found out the moment you swerve by a hair's breadth from perfection, whilst at the same time your work is so obvious, that everyone thinks it must be easy and puts you down as a duffer for botching it.

Shaw makes us see – almost hear – the great artists that are resurrected in his pages. Thus, on the entry of the statue in *Don Giovanni,* 'Maurel behaved very much as if his uncle had dropped in unexpectedly in the middle of a batchelor's supper-party'; and of Richter, playing 'The Ride of the Valkyries' immediately after the Prelude to *Parsifal,* 'To offer us such an orgie of scraping, screeching, banging, barking as a tone-picture of the daughters of Wotan was an outrage to Wagner.' He is trenchant when called for, generous when praise is deserved, sometimes unfair, occasionally silly. 'A more exasperatingly brainless composition was never put on paper', he writes of Schubert's great C major symphony, missing a quality greater than intellectual power. But one is almost glad to find Shaw fallible!

He loved music, and opera above all. Dan H. Laurence, in his recent edition of Shaw's criticisms, tells us: 'Even in his 94th year he continued to play and, quaveringly, to sing the scores of *Boris Godunov, Ariadne auf Naxos, The Dream of Gerontius.*' His mind remained open to the present, and it is significant that in his last published article (11 November 1950) he insisted that we sing better than our grandparents.

Pulborough, 1961   ALEC ROBERTSON

LONDON MUSIC IN
1888-9

Preface

✦✦

(1935)

WHEN my maiden novel, called Immaturity, was printed fifty years after it was written, I prefaced it with some account of the unhappy-go-lucky way in which I was brought up, ending with the nine years of shabby genteel destitution during which my attempts to gain a footing in literature were a complete and apparently hopeless failure.

I was rescued from this condition by William Archer, who transferred some of his book reviewing work to me, and pushed me into a post as picture critic which had been pushed on him, and for which he considered himself unqualified, as in fact he was. So, as reviewer for the old Pall Mall Gazette and picture critic for Edmund Yates's then fashionable weekly, The World, I carried on until I found an opening which I can explain only by describing the musical side of my childhood, to which I made only a passing allusion in my Immaturity preface, but which was of cardinal importance in my education.

In 1888, I being then thirty-two and already a noted critic and political agitator, the Star newspaper was founded under the editorship of the late T. P. O'Connor (nicknamed Tay Pay by Yates), who had for his very much more competent assistant the late H. W. Massingham. Tay Pay survived until 1936; but his mind never advanced beyond the year 1865, though his Fenian sympathies and his hearty detestation of the English nation disguised that defect from him. Massingham induced him to invite me to join the political staff of his paper; but as I had already, fourteen years before Lenin, read Karl Marx, and was preaching Socialism at every street corner or other available forum in London and the provinces, the effect of my articles on Tay Pay may be imagined. He refused to print them, and told me that, man alive, it would be five hundred years before such stuff would become practical political journalism. He was too goodnatured to sack me; and I did not want to throw away my job; so I got him out of his difficulty by asking him to let me have two columns a week for a feuilleton on music. He was glad to get rid of my politics on these terms; but he stipulated that – musical criticism being known to him only as unreadable and unintelligible jargon – I should, for God's sake, not write about Bach in B Minor. I was quite alive to that danger: in fact I had made my proposal because I believed I could make musical criticism readable even by the deaf. Besides, my terms were moderate: two guineas a week.

I was strong on the need for signed criticism written in the first person instead of the journalist 'we'; but as I then had no name worth signing, and G. B. S. meant nothing to the public, I had to invent a fantastic personality with something like a foreign title. I thought of Count di Luna (a character in Verdi's Trovatore), but finally changed it for Corno di Bassetto, as it sounded like a foreign title, and nobody knew what a corno di bassetto was.

As a matter of fact the corno di bassetto is not a foreigner with a title but a musical instrument called in English the basset horn. It is a wretched instrument, now completely snuffed out for general use by the bass clarionet. It would be forgotten and unplayed if it were not that Mozart has scored for it in his Requiem, evidently because its peculiar watery melancholy, and the total absence of any richness or passion in its tone, is just the thing for a funeral. Mendelssohn wrote some chamber music for it, presumably to oblige somebody who played it; and it is kept alive by these works and by our Mr Whall. If I had ever heard a note of it in 1888 I should not have selected it for a character which I intended to be sparkling. The devil himself could not make a basset horn sparkle.

For two years I sparkled every week in The Star under this ridiculous name, and in a manner so absolutely unlike the conventional musical criticism of the time that all the journalists believed that the affair was a huge joke, the point of which was that I knew nothing whatever about music. How it had come about that I was one of the few critics of that time who really knew their business I can explain only by picking up the thread of autobiography which I dropped in my scrappy prefix to Immaturity. For the sake of those who have not read the Immaturity preface, or have forgotten it, I shall have to repeat here some of my father's history, but only so far as is necessary to explain the situation of my mother.

Technically speaking I should say she was the worst mother conceivable, always, however, within the limits of the fact that she was incapable of unkindness to any child, animal, or flower, or indeed to any person or thing whatsoever. But if such a thing as a maternity welfare centre had been established or even imagined in Ireland in her time, and she had been induced to visit it, every precept of it would have been laughably strange to her. Though she had been severely educated up to the highest standard for Irish 'carriage ladies' of her time, she was much more like a Trobriand islander as described by Mr Malinowski than like a modern Cambridge lady graduate in respect of accepting all the habits, good or bad, of the Irish society in which she was brought up as part of an uncontrollable order of nature. She went her own way with so complete a disregard and even unconsciousness of convention and scandal and prejudice that it was impossible to doubt her good faith and innocence; but it never occurred to her that other people, especially children, needed guidance or training, or that it mattered in the least what they ate and drank or what they did as long as they were not actively mischievous. She accepted me as a natural and customary phenomenon, and took it for granted that I should go on occurring in that way. In short, living to her was not an art: it was something that happened. But there were unkind parts of it that could be avoided; and among these were the constraints and tyrannies, the scoldings and browbeatings and punishments she had suffered in her childhood as the method of her education. In her righteous reaction against it she reached a negative attitude in which, having no substitute to propose, she carried domestic anarchy as far as in the nature of things it can be carried.

She had been tyrannously taught French enough to recite one or two of Lafontaine's fables; to play the piano the wrong way; to harmonize by rule from Logier's Thoroughbass; to sit up straight and speak and dress and behave like a lady, and an Irish lady at that. She knew nothing of the value of money nor of housekeeping nor of hygiene nor of anything that could be left to servants or governesses or parents or solicitors or apothecaries or any other member of the retinue, indoor and outdoor, of a country house. She had great expectations from a humpbacked little aunt, a fairylike creature with a will of iron, who had brought up her motherless niece with a firm determination to make her a paragon of good breeding, to achieve a distinguished marriage for her, and to leave her all her money as a dowry.

Manufacturing destinies for other people is a dangerous game. Its results are usually as unexpected as those of a first-rate European war. When my mother came to marriageable age her long widowed father married again. The brother of his late wife, to whom he was considerably in debt, disapproved so strongly that on learning the date of the approaching ceremony from my mother he had the bridegroom arrested on his way to church. My grandfather naturally resented this manoeuvre, and in his wrath could not be persuaded that his daughter was not my grand-uncle's accomplice in it. Visits to relatives in Dublin provided a temporary refuge for her; and the affair would have blown over but for the intervention of my father.

My father was a very ineligible suitor for a paragon with great expectations. His family pretensions were enormous; but they were founded on many generations of younger sons, and were purely psychological. He had managed to acquire a gentlemanly post in the law courts. This post had been abolished and its holder pensioned. By selling the pension he was enabled to start in business as a wholesaler in the corn trade (retail trade was beneath his family dignity) of which he knew nothing. He accentuated this deficiency by becoming the partner of a Mr Clibborn, who had served an apprenticeship to the cloth trade. Their combined ignorances kept the business going, mainly by its own inertia, until they and it died. Many years after this event I paid a visit of curiosity to Jervis St Dublin; and there, on one of the pillars of a small portico, I found the ancient inscription 'Clibborn & Shaw' still decipherable, as it were on the tombs of the

Pharaohs. I cannot believe that this business yielded my father at any time more than three or four hundred a year; and it got less as time went on, as that particular kind of business was dying a slow death throughout the latter half of the nineteenth century.

My father was in principle an ardent teetotaller. Nobody ever felt the disgrace and misery and endless mischief of drunkenness as he did: he impressed it so deeply on me in my earliest years that I have been a teetotaller ever since. Unfortunately his conviction in this matter was founded on personal experience. He was the victim of a drink neurosis which cropped up in his family from time to time: a miserable affliction, quite unconvivial, and accompanied by torments of remorse and shame.

My father was past forty, and no doubt had sanguine illusions as to the future of his newly acquired business when he fell in love with my mother and was emboldened by her expectations and his business hopes to propose to her just at the moment when marriage seemed her only way of escape from an angry father and a stepmother. Immediately all her relatives, who had tolerated this middle-aged gentleman as a perfectly safe acquaintance with an agreeable vein of humor, denounced him as a notorious drunkard. My mother, suspicious of this sudden change of front, put the question directly to my father. His eloquence and sincerity convinced her that he was, as he claimed to be, and as he was in principle, a bigoted teetotaller. She married him; and her disappointed and infuriated aunt disinherited her, not foreseeing that the consequences of the marriage would include so remarkable a phenomenon as myself.

When my mother was disillusioned, and found out what living on a few hundreds a year with three children meant, even in a country where a general servant could be obtained for eight pounds a year, her condition must have been about as unhappy and her prospects as apparently hopeless as her aunt could have desired even in her most vindictive moments.

But there was one trump in her hand. She was fond of music, and had a mezzo-soprano voice of remarkable purity of tone. In the next street to ours, Harrington Street, where the houses were bigger and more fashionable than in our little by-street, there was a teacher of singing, lamed by an accident in childhood which had left one of his legs shorter than the other, but a man of mesmeric vitality and force. He was a bachelor living with his brother, whom he supported and adored, and a terrible old woman who was his servant of all work. His name was George John Vandaleur Lee, known in Dublin as Mr G. J. Lee. Singing lessons were cheap in Dublin; and my mother went to Lee to learn how to sing properly. He trained her voice to such purpose that she became indispensable to him as an amateur prima donna. For he was a most magnetic conductor and an indefatigable organizer of concerts, and later on of operas, with such amateur talent, vocal and orchestral, as he could discover and train in Dublin, which, as far as public professional music was concerned, was, outside the churches, practically a vacuum.

Lee soon found his way into our house, first by giving my mother lessons there, and then by using our drawing-room for rehearsals. I can only guess that the inadequacies of old Ellen in the Harrington Street house, and perhaps the incompatibilities of the brother, outweighed the comparative smallness of our house in Synge Street. My mother soon became not only prima donna and chorus leader but general musical factotum in the whirlpool of Lee's activity. Her grounding in Logier's Thoroughbass enabled her to take boundless liberties with composers. When authentic band parts were missing she thought nothing of making up an orchestral accompaniment of her own from the pianoforte score. Lee, as far as I know, had never seen a full orchestral score in his life: he conducted from a first violin part or from the vocal score, and had not, I think, any decided notion of orchestration as an idiosyncratic and characteristic part of a composer's work. He had no scholarship according to modern ideas; but he could do what Wagner said is the whole duty of a conductor: he could give the right time to the band; and he could pull it out of its amateur difficulties in emergencies by sheer mesmerism. Though he could not, or at any rate within my hearing never did sing a note, his taste in singing was classically perfect. In his search for the secret of *bel canto* he had gone to all the teachers within his reach. They told him that there was a voice in the head, a voice in the throat, and a voice in the chest. He dissected birds, and, with the connivance of medical friends, human subjects, in his search for these three organs. He then told the teachers authoritatively that the three voices were fabulous, and that the voice was produced by a single instrument called the larynx. They replied that musical art had nothing to do with anatomy, and that for a musician to practise dissection was unheard-of and disgusting. But as, tested by results, their efforts to teach their pupils to screech like locomotive whistles not only outraged his ear but wrecked the voices and often the health of their victims, their practice was as unacceptable to him as their theory.

Thus Lee became the enemy of every teacher of singing in Dublin; and they reciprocated heartily. In this negative attitude he was left until, at the opera, he heard an Italian baritone named Badeali, who at the age of eighty, when he first discovered these islands, had a perfectly preserved voice, and, to Lee's taste, a perfectly produced one. Lee, thanks to his dissections, listened with a clear knowledge of what a larynx is really like. The other vocal organs and their action were obvious and conscious. Guided by this knowledge, and by his fine ear, his fastidious taste, and his instinct, he found out what Badeali was doing when he was singing. The other teachers were interested in Badeali only because one of his accomplishments was to drink a glass of wine and sing a sustained note at the same time. Finally Lee equipped himself with a teaching method which became a religion for him: the only religion, I may add, he ever professed. And my mother, as his pupil, learnt and embraced this musical faith, and rejected all other creeds as uninteresting superstitions. And it did not fail her; for she lived to be Badeali's age and kept her voice without a scrape on it until the end.

I have to dwell on The Method, as we called it in the family, because my mother's association with Lee, and the *ménage à trois* in which it resulted, would be unpleasantly misunderstood without this clue to it. For after the death of Lee's brother, which affected him to the verge of suicide, we left our respective houses and went to live in the same house, number one Hatch Street, which was half in Lower Leeson Street. The arrangement was economical; for we could not afford to live in a fashionable house, and Lee could not afford to give lessons in an unfashionable one, though, being a bachelor, he needed only a music room and a bedroom. We also shared a cottage in Dalkey, high up on Torca Hill, with all Dublin Bay from Dalkey Island to Howth visible from the garden, and all Killiney Bay with the Wicklow mountains in the background from the hall door. Lee bought this cottage and presented it to my mother, though she never had any legal claim to it and did not benefit by its sale later on. It was not conveniently situated for rehearsals or lessons; but there were musical neighbors who allowed me to some extent to run in and out of their houses when there was music going on.

The *ménage à trois*, alternating between Hatch St and Dalkey, worked in its ramshackle way quite smoothly until I was fifteen or thereabouts, when Lee went to London and our family broke up into fragments that never got pieced together again.

In telling the story so far, I have had to reconstruct the part of it which occurred before I came into it and began, as my nurse put it, to take notice. I can remember the ante-Lee period in Synge St when my father, as sole chief of the household, read family prayers and formally admitted that we had done those things which we ought not to have done and left undone those things which we ought to have done, which was certainly true as far as I was personally concerned. He added that there was no health in us; and this also was true enough about myself; for Dr Newland, our apothecary, was in almost continual attendance to administer cathartics; and when I had a sore throat I used to hold out for sixpence before submitting to a mustard plaster round my neck. We children (I had two sisters older than myself and no brothers) were abandoned entirely to the servants, who, with the exception of Nurse Williams, who was a good and honest woman, were utterly unfit to be trusted with the charge of three cats, much less three children. I had my meals in the kitchen, mostly of stewed beef, which I loathed, badly cooked potatoes, sound or diseased as the case might be, and much too much tea out of brown delft teapots left to 'draw' on the hob until it was pure tannin. Sugar I stole. I was never hungry, because my father, often insufficiently fed in his childhood, had such a horror of child hunger that he insisted on unlimited bread and butter being always within our reach. When I was troublesome a servant thumped me on the head until one day, greatly daring, I rebelled, and, on finding her collapse abjectly, became thenceforth uncontrollable. I hated the servants and liked my mother because, on the one or two rare and delightful occasions when she buttered my bread for me, she buttered it thickly instead of merely wiping a knife on it. Her almost complete neglect of me had the advantage that I could idolize her to the utmost pitch of my imagination and had no sordid or disillusioning contacts with her. It was a privilege to be taken for a walk or a visit with her, or on an excursion.

My ordinary exercise whilst I was still too young to be allowed out by myself was to be taken out by a servant, who was supposed to air me on the banks of the canal or round the fashionable squares where the atmosphere was esteemed salubrious and the surroundings gentlemanly. Actually she took me into the slums to visit her private friends, who dwelt in squalid tenements. When she met a generous male acquaintance who insisted on treating her she took me into the public house bars, where I was regaled with lemonade and gingerbeer; but I did not enjoy these treats, because my father's eloquence on the evil of drink had given me an impression that a public house was a wicked place into which I should not have been taken. Thus were laid the foundations of my lifelong hatred of poverty, and the devotion of all my public life to the task of exterminating the poor and rendering their resurrection for ever impossible.

Note, by the way, that I should have been much more decently brought up if my parents had been too poor to afford servants.

As to early education I can remember our daily governess, Miss Hill, a needy lady who seemed to me much older than she can really have been. She puzzled me with her attempts to teach me to read; for I can remember no time at which a page of print was not intelligible to me, and can only suppose that I was born literate. She tried to give me and my two sisters a taste for poetry by reciting 'Stop; for thy tread is on an empire's dust' at us, and only succeeded, poor lady, in awakening our sense of derisive humor. She punished me by little strokes with her fingers that would not have discomposed a fly, and even persuaded me that I ought to cry and feel disgraced on such occasions. She gave us judgment books and taught us to feel jubilant when after her departure we could rush to the kitchen crying 'No marks today' and to hang back ashamed when this claim could not be substantiated. She taught me to add, subtract, and multiply, but could not teach me division, because she kept saying two into four, three into six, and so forth without ever explaining what the word 'into' meant in this connection. This was explained to me on my first day at school; and I solemnly declare that it was the only thing I ever learnt at school. However, I must not complain; for my immurement in that damnable boy prison effected its real purpose of preventing my being a nuisance to my mother at home for at least half the day.

The only other teaching I had was from my clerical Uncle William George (surnamed Carroll) who, being married to one of my many maternal aunts (my father had no end of brothers and sisters), had two boys of his own to educate, and took me on with them for awhile in the early mornings to such purpose that when his lessons were ended by my being sent to school, I knew more Latin grammar than any other boy in the First Latin Junior, to which I was relegated. After a few years in that establishment I had forgotten most of it, and, as aforesaid, learnt nothing; for there was only the thinnest pretence of teaching anything but Latin and Greek, if asking a boy once a day in an overcrowded class the Latin for a man or a horse or what not, can be called teaching him Latin. I was far too busy educating myself out of school by reading every book I could lay my hands on, and clambering all over Killiney hill looking at the endless pictures nature painted for me, meanwhile keeping my mind busy by telling myself all sorts of stories, to puzzle about my vocabulary lesson, as the punishments were as futile as the teaching. At the end of my schooling I knew nothing of what the school professed to teach; but I was a highly educated boy all the same. I could sing and whistle from end to end leading works by Handel, Haydn, Mozart, Beethoven, Rossini, Bellini, Donizetti, and Verdi. I was saturated with English literature, from Shakespear and Bunyan to Byron and Dickens. And I was so susceptible to natural beauty that, having had some glimpse of the Dalkey scenery on an excursion, I still remember the moment when my mother told me that we were going to live there as the happiest of my life.

And all this I owed to the meteoric impact of Lee, with his music, his method, his impetuous enterprise and his magnetism, upon the little Shaw household where a thoroughly disgusted and disillusioned woman was suffering from a hopelessly disappointing husband and three uninteresting children grown too old to be petted like the animals and birds she was so fond of, to say nothing of the humiliating inadequacy of my father's income. We never felt any affection for Lee; for he was too excessively unlike us, too completely a phenomenon, to rouse any primitive human feeling in us. When my mother introduced him to me, he played with me for the first and last time; but as his notion of play was to decorate my face with moustaches and whiskers in burnt cork in spite of the most furious resistance I could put up, our encounter was not a success; and the defensive attitude in which it left me lasted, though without the least bitterness, until the decay of his energies and the growth of mine put us on more than equal terms. He never read anything except Tyndall on Sound, which he kept in his bedroom for years. He complained that an edition of Shakespear which I lent him was incomplete because it did not contain The School for Scandal, which for some reason he wanted to read; and when I talked of Carlyle he understood me to mean the Viceroy of that name who had graciously attended his concerts in the Antient Concert Rooms. Although he supplanted my father as the dominant factor in the household, and appropriated all the activity and interest of my mother, he was so completely absorbed in his musical affairs that there was no friction and hardly any intimate personal contacts between the two men: certainly no unpleasantness. At first his ideas astonished us. He said that people should sleep with their windows open. The daring of this appealed to me; and I have done so ever since. He ate brown bread instead of white: a startling eccentricity. He had no faith in doctors, and when my mother had a serious illness took her case in hand unhesitatingly and at the end of a week or so gave my trembling father leave to call in a leading Dublin doctor, who simply said 'My work is done' and took his hat. As to the apothecary and his squills, he could not exist in Lee's atmosphere; and I was never attended by a doctor again until I caught the smallpox in the epidemic of 1881. He took no interest in pictures or in any art but his own; and even in music his interest was limited to vocal music: I did not know that such things as string quartets or symphonies existed until I began, at sixteen, to investigate music for myself. Beethoven's sonatas and the classical operatic overtures were all I knew of what Wagner called absolute music. I should be tempted to say that none of us knew of the existence of Bach were it not that my mother sang My Heart Ever Faithful, the banjo like obbligato of which amused me very irreverently.

Lee was like all artists whose knowledge is solely a working knowledge: there were holes in his culture which I had to fill up for myself. Fortunately his richer pupils sometimes presented him with expensive illustrated books. He never opened them; but I did. He was so destitute of any literary bent that when he published a book entitled The Voice, it was written for him by a scamp of a derelict doctor whom he entertained for that purpose, just as in later years his prospectuses and press articles were written by me. He never visited the Dublin National Gallery, one of the finest collections of its size in Europe, with the usual full set of casts from what was called the antique, meaning ancient Greek sculpture. It was by prowling in this gallery that I learnt to recognize the work of the old masters at sight. I learnt French history from the novels of Dumas père, and English history from Shakespear and Walter Scott. Good boys were meanwhile learning lessons out of schoolbooks and receiving marks at examinations: a process which left them pious barbarians whilst I was acquiring an equipment which enabled me not only to pose as Corno di Bassetto when the chance arrived, but to add the criticism of pictures to the various strings I had to my bow as a feuilletonist.

Meanwhile nobody ever dreamt of teaching me anything. At fifteen, when the family broke up, I could neither play nor read a note of music. Whether you choose to put it that I was condemned to be a critic or saved from being an executant, the fact remains that when the house became musicless, I was forced to teach myself how to play written music on the piano from a book with a diagram of the keyboard in it or else be starved of music.

Not that I wanted to be a professional musician. My ambition was to be a great painter like Michael Angelo (one of my heroes); but my attempts to obtain instruction in his art at the School of Design presided over by the South Kensington Department of Science and Art only prevented me from learning anything except how to earn five shilling grants for the masters (payment by results) by filling up ridiculous examination papers in practical geometry and what they called freehand drawing.

With competent instruction I daresay I could have become a painter and draughtsman of sorts; but the School of Design convinced me that I was a hopeless failure in that direction on no better ground than that I found I could not draw like Michael Angelo or paint like Titian at the first attempt without knowing how. But teaching, of art and everything else, was and still is so little understood by our professional instructors (mostly themselves failures) that only the readymade geniuses make good; and even they are as often as not the worse for their academic contacts.

As an alternative to being a Michael Angelo I had dreams of being a Badeali. (Note, by the way, that of literature I had no dreams at all, any more than a duck has of swimming.) What that led to was not fully explained until Matthias Alexander, in search, like Lee, of a sound vocal method, invented his technique of self-control.

I had sung like a bird all through my childhood; but when my voice broke I at once fell into the error unmasked by Alexander of trying to gain my end before I had studied the means. In my attempts to reproduce the frenzies of the Count di Luna, the

sardonic accents of Gounod's Mephistopheles, the noble charm
of Don Giovanni, and the supernatural menace of the Com-
mendatore, not to mention all the women's parts and the tenor
parts as well (for all parts, high or low, male or female, had to
be sung or shrieked or whistled or growled somehow) I thought
of nothing but the dramatic characters; and in attacking them I
set my jaws and my glottis as if I had to crack walnuts with
them. I might have ruined my voice if I had not imitated good
singers instead of bad ones; but even so the results were wretched.
When I rejoined my mother in London and she found that I had
taught myself to play accompaniments and to amuse myself with
operas and oratorios as other youths read novels and smoke
cigarets, she warned me that my voice would be spoiled if I went
on like that. Thereupon I insisted on being shewn the proper
way to sing. The instructive result was that when, following my
mother's directions, I left my jaw completely loose, and my
tongue flat instead of convulsively rolling it up; when I operated
my diaphragm so as to breathe instead of 'blowing'; when I
tried to round up my pharynx and soft palate and found it like
trying to wag my ears, I found that for the first time in my life
I could not produce an audible note. It seemed that I had no
voice. But I believed in Lee's plan and knew that my own was
wrong. I insisted on being taught how to use my voice as if I had
one; and in the end the unused and involuntary pharyngeal
muscles became active and voluntary, and I developed an uninteresting baritone voice of no exceptional range which I have
ever since used for my private satisfaction and exercise without
damaging either it or myself in the process.

Here I must digress for a moment to point a moral. Years after
I learnt how to sing without spoiling my voice and wrecking my
general health, a musician-reciter (Matthias Alexander aforesaid)
found himself disabled by the complaint known as clergyman's
sore throat. Having the true scientific spirit and industry, he set
himself to discover what it was that he was really doing to dis-
able himself in this fashion by his efforts to produce the opposite
result. In the end he found this out, and a great deal more as
well. He established not only the beginnings of a far reaching

science of the apparently involuntary movements we call reflexes, but a technique of correction and selfcontrol which forms a substantial addition to our very slender resources in personal education.

Meanwhile a Russian doctor named Pavlov devoted himself to the investigation of the same subject by practising the horrible voodoo into which professional medical research had lapsed in the nineteenth century. For quarter of a century he tormented and mutilated dogs most abominably, and finally wrote a ponderous treatise on reflexes in which he claimed to have established on a scientific basis the fact that a dog's mouth will water at the sound of a dinner bell when it is trained to associate that sound with a meal, and that dogs, if tormented, thwarted, baffled, and incommoded continuously, will suffer nervous breakdown and be miserably ruined for the rest of their lives. He was also able to describe what happens to a dog when half its brains are cut out.

What his book and its shamefully respectful reception by professional biologists does demonstrate is that the opening of the scientific professions to persons qualified for them neither by general capacity nor philosophic moral training plunges professional Science, as it has so often plunged professional Religion and Jurisprudence, into an abyss of stupidity and cruelty from which nothing but the outraged humanity of the laity can rescue it.

In the department of biology especially, the professors, mostly brought up as Fundamentalists, are informed that the book of Genesis is not a scientific document, and that the tribal idol whom Noah conciliated by the smell of roast meat is not God and never had any objective existence. They absurdly infer that the pursuit of scientific knowledge: that is, of all knowledge, is exempt from moral obligations, and consequently that they are privileged as scientists to commit the most revolting cruelties when they are engaged in research.

Their next step in this crazy logic is that no research is scientific unless it involves such cruelties. With all the infinite possibilities of legitimate and kindly research open to anyone with enough industry and ingenuity to discover innocent methods of exploration, they set up a boycott of brains and a ritual of sacrifice of dogs and guinea pigs which impresses the superstitious public as all such rituals do. Thereby they learn many things that no decent person ought to know; for it must not be forgotten that human advancement consists not only of adding to the store of human knowledge and experience but eliminating much that is burdensome and brutish. Our forefathers had the knowledge and experience gained by seeing heretics burnt at the stake and harlots whipped through the streets at the cart's tail. Mankind is better without such knowledge and experience.

If Pavlov had been a poacher he would have been imprisoned for his cruelty and despised for his moral imbecility. But as Director of the Physiological Department of the Institute of Experimental Medicine at St Petersburg, and Professor of the Medical Academy, he was virtually forced to mutilate and torment dogs instead of discovering the methods by which humane unofficial investigators were meanwhile finding out all that he was looking for.

The reaction against this voodoo is gathering momentum; but still our rich philanthropic industrialists lavish millions on the endowment of research without taking the most obvious precautions against malversation of their gifts for the benefit of dog stealers, guinea pig breeders, laboratory builders and plumbers, and a routine of cruel folly and scoundrelism that perverts and wastes all the scientific enthusiasm that might otherwise have by this time reduced our death and disease rates to their natural minimum. I am sorry to have to describe so many highly respected gentlemen quite deliberately as fools and scoundrels; but the only definition of scoundrelism known to me is anarchism in morals; and I cannot admit that the hackneyed pleas of the dynamiter and the assassin in politics become valid in the laboratory and the hospital, or that the man who thinks they do is made any less a fool by calling him a professor of physiology.

And all this because in 1860 the men who thought they wanted to substitute scientific knowledge for superstition really wanted only to abolish God and marry their deceased wives' sisters!

I should add that there is no reason to suppose that Pavlov was by nature a bad man. He bore a strong external resemblance to myself, and was wellmeaning, intelligent, and devoted to science. It was his academic environment that corrupted, stultified, and sterilized him. If only he had been taught to sing by my mother no dog need ever have collapsed in terror at his approach; and he might have shared the laurels of Alexander.

And now I must return to my story. Lee's end was more tragic than Pavlov's. I do not know at what moment he began to deteriorate. He was a sober and moderate liver in all respects; and he was never ill until he treated himself to a tour in Italy and caught malaria there. He fought through it without a doctor on cold water, and returned apparently well; but whenever he worked too hard it came back and prostrated him for a day or two. Finally his ambition undid him. Dublin in those days seemed a hopeless place for an artist; for no success counted except a London success. The summit of a provincial conductor's destiny was to preside at a local musical festival modelled on the Three Choirs or Handel Festivals. Lee declared that he would organize and conduct a Dublin Festival with his own chorus and with all the famous leading singers from the Italian opera in London. This he did in connection with an Exhibition in Dublin. My mother, of course, led the chorus. At a rehearsal the contralto, Madame de Meric Lablache, took exception to something and refused to sing. Lee shrugged his shoulders and asked my mother to carry on, which she did to such purpose that Madame Lablache took care not to give her another such chance.

At the Festivals Lee reached the Dublin limit of eminence. Nothing remained but London. He was assured that London meant a very modest beginning all over again, and perhaps something of an established position after fifteen years or so. Lee said that he would take a house in Park Lane, then the most exclusive and expensive thoroughfare in the west end, sacred to peers and millionaires, and – stupendous on the scale of Irish finance – make his pupils pay him a guinea a lesson. And this he actually did with a success that held out quite brilliantly for several seasons and then destroyed him. For whereas he had succeeded in Dublin by the sheer superiority of his method and talent and character, training his pupils honestly for a couple of years to sing beautifully and classically, he found that the London ladies who took him up so gushingly would have none of his beauty and classicism, and would listen to nothing less than a promise to make them sing 'like Patti' in twelve lessons. It was that or starve.

He submitted perforce; but he was no longer the same man, the man to whom all circumstances seemed to give way, and who made his own musical world and reigned in it. He had even to change his name and his aspect. G. L. Lee, with the black whiskers and the clean shaven resolute lip and chin, became Vandaleur Lee, whiskerless, but with a waxed and pointed moustache and an obsequious attitude. It suddenly became evident that he was an elderly man, and, to those who had known him in Dublin, a humbug. Performances of Marchetti's Ruy Blas with my sister as the Queen of Spain, and later on of Sullivan's Patience and scraps of Faust and Il Trovatore were achieved; but musical society in London at last got tired of the damaged Svengali who could manufacture Pattis for twelve guineas; and the guineas ceased to come in. Still, as there were no night clubs in those days, it was possible to let a house in Park Lane for the night to groups of merrymakers; and Lee was holding out there without pupils when he asked me to draft a circular for him announcing that he could cure clergyman's sore throat. He was still at Park Lane when he dropped dead in the act of undressing himself, dying as he had lived, without a doctor. The postmortem and inquest revealed the fact that his brain was diseased and had been so for a long time. I was glad to learn that his decay was pathological as well as ecological, and that the old efficient and honest Lee had been real after all. But I took to heart the lesson in the value of London fashionable successes. To this day I look to the provincial and the amateur for honesty and genuine fecundity in art.

Meanwhile, what had happened to the *ménage à trois*? and how did I turn up in Park Lane playing accompaniments and getting glimpses of that artstruck side of fashionable society which takes refuge in music from the routine of politics and sport which occupies the main Philistine body?

Well, when Lee got his foot in at a country house in Shropshire whither he had been invited to conduct some private performances, he sold the Dalkey cottage and concluded his tenancy of Hatch Street. This left us in a house which we could afford less than ever; for my father's moribund business was by now considerably deader than it had been at the date of my birth. My younger sister was dying of consumption caught from reckless contacts at a time when neither consumption nor pneumonia were regarded as catching. All that could be done was to recommend a change of climate. My elder sister had a beautiful voice. In the last of Lee's Dublin adventures in amateur opera she had appeared as Amina in Bellini's La Sonnambula, on which occasion the tenor lost his place and his head, and Lucy obligingly sang most of his part as well as her own. Unfortunately her musical endowment was so complete that it cost her no effort to sing or play anything she had once heard, or to read any music at sight. She simply could not associate the idea of real work with music; and as in any case she had never received any sort of training, her very facility prevented her from becoming a serious artist, though, as she could sing difficult music without breaking her voice, she got through a considerable share of public singing in her time.

Now neither my mother nor any of us knew how much more is needed for an opera singer than a voice and natural musicianship. It seemed to us that as, after a rehearsal or two, she could walk on to the stage, wave her arms about in the absurd manner then in vogue in opera, and sing not only her own part but everybody else's as well, she was quite qualified to take the place of Christine Nilsson or Adelina Patti if only she could get a proper introduction. And clearly Lee, now in the first flush of his success in Park Lane, would easily be able to secure this for her.

There was another resource. My now elderly mother believed that she could renounce her amateur status and make a living in London by teaching singing. Had she not the infallible Method to impart? So she realized a little of the scrap of settled property of which her long deceased aunt had not been able to deprive her; sold the Hatch Street furniture; settled my father and myself in comfortable lodgings at 61 Harcourt St; and took my sisters to the Isle of Wight, where the younger one died. She then took a semi-detached villa in a *cul-de-sac* off the Fulham Road, and waited there for Lucy's plans and her own to materialize.

The result was almost a worse disillusion than her marriage. That had been cured by Lee's music: besides, my father had at last realized his dream of being a practising teetotaller, and was now as inoffensive an old gentleman as any elderly wife could desire. It was characteristic of the Shavian drink neurosis to vanish suddenly in this way. But that Lee should be unfaithful! unfaithful to The Method! that he, the one genuine teacher among so many quacks, should now stoop to outquack them all and become a moustachioed charlatan with all the virtue gone out of him: this was the end of all things; and she never forgave it. She was not unkind: she tolerated Lee the charlatan as she had tolerated Shaw the dipsomaniac because, as I guess, her early motherless privation of affection and her many disappointments in other people had thrown her back on her own considerable internal resources and developed her self-sufficiency and power of solitude to an extent which kept her up under circumstances that would have crushed or embittered any woman who was the least bit of a clinger. She dropped Lee very gently: at first he came and went at Victoria Grove, Fulham Road; and she went and came at 13 Park Lane, helping with the music there at his At Homes, and even singing the part of Donna Anna for him (elderly prima donnas were then tolerated as matters of course) at an amateur performance of Don Giovanni. But my sister, who had quarrelled with him as a child when he tried to give her piano lessons, and had never liked him, could not bear him at all in his new phase, and, when she found that he could not really advance her prospects of becoming a prima donna, broke with him completely and made it difficult for him to continue his visits. When he died we had not seen him for some years; and my mother did not display the slightest emotion at the news. He had been dead for her ever since he had ceased to be an honest teacher of singing and a mesmeric conductor.

Her plans for herself came almost to nothing for several years. She found that Englishwomen do not wish to be made to sing beautifully and classically: they want to sing erotically; and this my mother thought not only horrible but unladylike. Her love songs were those of Virginia Gabriel and Arthur Sullivan, all about bereaved lovers and ending with a hope for reunion in the next world. She could sing with perfect purity of tone and touching expression

> Oh, Ruby, my darling, the small white hand
> Which gathered the harebell was never my own.

But if you had been able to anticipate the grand march of human progress and poetic feeling by fifty years, and asked her to sing

> You made me love you.
> I didn't want to do it.
> I didn't want to do it,

she would have asked a policeman to remove you to a third-class carriage.

Besides, though my mother was not consciously a snob, the divinity which hedged an Irish lady of her period was not acceptable to the British suburban parents, all snobs, who were within her reach. They liked to be treated with deference; and it never occurred to my mother that such people could entertain a pretension so monstrous in her case. Her practice with private pupils was negligible until she was asked to become musical instructress at the North London College. Her success was immediate; for not only did her classes leave the other schools nowhere musically, but the divinity aforesaid exactly suited her new rôle as schoolmistress. Other schools soon sought her services; and she remained in request until she insisted on retiring on the ground that her age made her public appearances ridiculous. By that time all the old money troubles were over and forgotten, as my financial position enabled me to make her perfectly comfortable in that respect.

And now, what about myself, the incipient Corno di Bassetto? Well, when my mother sold the Hatch Street furniture, it never occurred to her to sell our piano, though I could not play it, nor could my father. We did not realize, nor did she, that she was never coming back, and that, except for a few days when my father, taking a little holiday for the first time in his life within my experience, came to see us in London, she would never meet him again. Family revolutions would seldom be faced if they did not present themselves at first as temporary makeshifts. Accordingly, having lived since my childhood in a house full of music, I suddenly found myself in a house where there was no music, and could be none unless I made it myself. I have recorded elsewhere how, having purchased one of Weale's Handbooks which contained a diagram of the keyboard and an explanation of musical notation, I began my self-tuition, not with Czerny's five-finger exercises, but with the overture to Don Giovanni, thinking rightly that I had better start with something I knew well enough to hear whether my fingers were on the right notes or not. There were plenty of vocal scores of operas and oratorios in our lodging; and although I never acquired any technical skill as a pianist, and cannot to this day play a scale with any certainty of not foozling it, I acquired what I wanted: the power to take a vocal score and learn its contents as if I heard it rehearsed by my mother and her colleagues. I could manage arrangements of orchestral music much better than piano music proper. At last I could play the old rum-tum accompaniments of those days well enough (knowing how they *should* be played) to be more agreeable to singers than many really competent pianists. I bought more scores, among them one of Lohengrin, through which I made the revolutionary discovery of Wagner. I bought arrangements of Beethoven's symphonies, and discovered the musical regions that lie outside opera and oratorio. Later on, I was forced to learn to play the classical symphonies and overtures in strict time by hammering the bass in piano duets with my sister in London. I played Bach's Inventions and his Art of Fugue. I studied academic textbooks, and actually worked out exercises in harmony and counterpoint under supervision by an organist friend named Crament, avoiding consecutive fifths and octaves, and having not the faintest notion of what the result would sound like. I read pseudo-scientific treatises about the roots of chords which candidates for the degree of Mus. Doc. at the universities had to swallow, and learnt that Stainer's commonsense views would get you plucked at Oxford, and Ouseley's pedantries at Cambridge. I read Mozart's Succinct Thoroughbass (a scrap of paper with some helpful tips on it which he scrawled for his pupil Sussmaier); and this, many years later, Edward Elgar told me was the only document in existence of the smallest use to a student composer. It was, I grieve to say, of no use to me; but then I was not a young composer. It ended in my knowing much more about music than any of the great composers, an easy achievement for any critic, however barren. For awhile I must have become a little pedantic; for I remember being shocked, on looking up Lee's old vocal score of Don Giovanni, to find that he had cut out all the repetitions which Mozart had perpetrated as a matter of sonata form. I now see that Lee was a century before his time in this reform, and hope some day to hear a performance of Mozart's Idomeneo in which nothing is sung twice over.

When I look back on all the banging, whistling, roaring, and growling inflicted on nervous neighbors during this process of education, I am consumed with useless remorse. But what else could I have done? Today there is the wireless, which enables me to hear from all over Europe more good music in a week than I could then hear in ten years, if at all. When, after my five years office slavery, I joined my mother in London and lived with her for twenty years until my marriage, I used to drive her nearly crazy by my favorite selections from Wagner's Ring, which to her was 'all recitative', and horribly discordant at that. She never complained at the time, but confessed it after we separated, and said that she had sometimes gone away to cry. If I had committed a murder I do not think it would trouble my conscience very much; but this I cannot bear to think of. If I had to live my life over again I should devote it to the establishment of some arrangement of headphones and microphones or the like whereby the noises made by musical maniacs should be audible to themselves only. In Germany it is against the law to play the piano with the window open. But of what use is that to the people in the house? It should be made felony to play a musical instrument in any other than a completely soundproof room. The same should apply to loud speakers on pain of confiscation.

Readers with a taste for autobiography must now take my Immaturity preface and dovetail it into this sketch to complete the picture. My business here is to account for my proposal to Tay Pay and my creation of Bassetto. From my earliest recorded sign of an interest in music when as a small child I encored my mother's singing of the page's song from the first act of Les Huguenots (note that I shared Herbert Spencer's liking for Meyerbeer) music has been an indispensable part of my life. Harley Granville-Barker was not far out when, at a rehearsal of one of my plays, he cried out 'Ladies and gentlemen: will you please remember that this is Italian opera.'

I reprint Bassetto's stuff shamefacedly after long hesitation with a reluctance which has been overcome only by my wife, who has found some amusement in reading it through, a drudgery which I could not bring myself to undertake. I know it was great fun when it was fresh, and that many people have a curious antiquarian taste (I have it myself) for old chronicles of dead musicians and actors. I must warn them, however, not to expect to find here the work of the finished critic who wrote my volumes entitled Music in London, 1890–94, and Our Theatres in the Nineties. I knew all that was necessary about music; but in criticism I was only a beginner. It is easy enough from the first to distinguish between what is pleasant or unpleasant, accurate or inaccurate in a performance; but when great artists have to be dealt with, only keenly analytical observation and comparison of them with artists who, however agreeable, are not great, can enable a critic to distinguish between what everybody can do and what only a very few can do, and to get his valuations right accordingly. All artsmen know what it is to be enthusiastically praised for something so easy that they are half ashamed of it, and to receive not a word of encouragement for their finest strokes.

I cannot deny that Bassetto was occasionally vulgar; but that does not matter if he makes you laugh. Vulgarity is a necessary part of a complete author's equipment; and the clown is sometimes the best part of the circus. The Star, then a hapenny newspaper, was not catering for a fastidious audience: it was addressed to the bicycle clubs and the polytechnics, not to the Royal Society of Literature or the Musical Association. I purposely vulgarized musical criticism, which was then refined and academic to the point of being unreadable and often nonsensical. Editors, being mostly ignorant of music, would submit to anything from their musical critics, not pretending to understand it. If I occasionally carried to the verge of ribaldry my reaction against the pretentious twaddle and sometimes spiteful cliquishness they tolerated in their ignorance, think of me as heading one of the pioneer columns of what was then called The New Journalism; and you will wonder at my politeness.

You may be puzzled, too, to find that the very music I was brought up on: the pre-Wagner school of formal melody in separate numbers which seemed laid out to catch the encores that were then fashionable, was treated by me with contemptuous levity as something to be swept into the dustbin as soon as possible. The explanation is that these works were standing in the way of Wagner, who was then the furiously abused coming man in London. Only his early works were known or tolerated. Half a dozen bars of Tristan or The Mastersingers made professional musicians put their fingers in their ears. The Ride of the Valkyries was played at the Promenade Concerts, and always encored, but only as an insanely rampagious curiosity. The Daily Telegraph steadily preached Wagner down as a discordant notoriety-hunting charlatan in six silk dressing-gowns, who could not write a bar of melody, and made an abominable noise with the orchestra. In pantomime harlequinades the clown produced a trombone, played a bit of the pilgrims' march from Tannhäuser fortissimo as well as he could, and said 'The music of the future!' The wars of religion were not more bloodthirsty than the discussions of the Wagnerites and the Anti-Wagnerites. I was, of course, a violent Wagnerite; and I had the advantage of knowing the music to which Wagner grew up, whereas many of the most fanatical Wagnerites (Ashton Ellis, who translated the Master's prose works, was a conspicuous example) knew no other music than Wagner's, and believed that the music of Donizetti and Meyerbeer had no dramatic quality whatever. 'A few arpeggios' was the description Ellis gave me of his notion of Les Huguenots.

Nowadays the reaction is all the other way. Our young lions have no use for Wagner the Liberator. His harmonies, which once seemed monstrous cacophonies, are the commonplaces of the variety theatres. Audacious young critics disparage his grandeurs as tawdry. When the wireless strikes up the Tannhäuser overture I hasten to switch it off, though I can always listen with pleasure to Rossini's overture to William Tell, hackneyed to death in Bassetto's time. The funeral march from Die Götterdämmerung hardly keeps my attention, though Handel's march from Saul is greater than ever. Though I used to scarify the fools who said that Wagner's music was formless, I should not now think the worse of Wagner if, like Bach and Mozart, he had combined the most poignant dramatic expression with the most elaborate decorative design. It was necessary for him to smash the superstition that this was obligatory; to free dramatic melody from the tyranny of arabesques; and to give the orchestra symphonic work instead of rosalias and rum-tum; but now that this and all the other musical superstitions are in the dustbin, and the post-Wagnerian harmonic and contrapuntal anarchy is so complete that it is easier technically to compose another Parsifal than another Bach's Mass in B Minor or Don Giovanni I am no longer a combatant anarchist in music, not to mention that I have learnt that a successful revolution's first task is to shoot all revolutionists. This means that I am no longer Corno di Bassetto. He was pre- and pro-Wagner; unfamiliar with Brahms; and unaware that a young musician named Elgar was chuckling over his irreverent boutades. As to Cyril Scott, Bax, Ireland, Goossens, Bliss, Walton, Schönberg, Hindemith, or even Richard Strauss and Sibelius, their idioms would have been quite outside Bassetto's conception of music, though today they seem natural enough. Therefore I very greatly doubt whether poor old Bassetto is worth reading now. Still, you are not compelled to read him. Having read the preface you can shut the book and give it to your worst enemy as a birthday present.

Mid-Atlantic
Sunday, 2 June 1935

Dido at Bow

✢

21 February 1889

ON Monday the editor of The Star summoned me to a private conference. 'The fact is, my dear Corno,' he said, throwing himself back in his chair and arranging his moustache with the diamond which sparkles at the end of his pen-handle, 'I don't believe that music in London is confined to St James's Hall, Covent Garden, and the Albert Hall. People must sing and play elsewhere. Whenever I go down to speak at the big Town Halls at Shoreditch, Hackney, Stratford, Holborn, Kensington, Battersea, and deuce knows where, I always see bills at the door announcing oratorios, organ recitals, concerts by local Philharmonic and Orpheus societies, and all sorts of musical games. Why not criticise these instead of saying the same thing over and over again about Henschel and Richter and Norman Neruda and the rest?' I replied, as best I could, that my experience as a musical critic had left me entirely unacquainted with these outlandish localities and their barbarous minstrelsy; that I regarded London as bounded on the extreme north-east by Stonecutter Street, on the extreme south-west by Kensington Gore, on the south by the Thames, and on the north by the Strand and Regent-street. He assured me that the places he had mentioned actually existed; but that, as I was evidently hurt by the suggestion that I should condescend to visit them, he would hand the ticket he had just received for a Purcell–Handel performance at Bow, to Musigena. 'What!' I exclaimed, 'Purcell! the greatest of English composers, left to Musigena! to a man whose abnormal gifts in every other direction have blinded him to his utter ignorance of music!' 'Well, the fact is' said the editor 'Musigena told me only half an hour ago that he was at a loss to imagine how a writer so profound and accomplished as di Bassetto could be in music a mere superficial amateur.' I waited to hear no more. Snatching the tickets from the editor's desk, I hastily ran home to get my revolver as a precaution during my hazardous voyage to the east end. Then I dashed away to Broad-street, and asked the booking-clerk whether he knew of a place called Bow. He was evidently a man of extraordinary nerve, for he handed me a ticket without any sign of surprise, as if a voyage to Bow were the most commonplace event possible. A little later the train was rushing through the strangest places: Shoreditch, of which I had read in historical novels; Old Ford, which I had supposed to be a character in one of Shakespeare's plays; Homerton, which is somehow associated in my mind with pigeons; and Haggerston, a name perfectly new to me. When I got into the concert-room I was perfectly dazzled by the appearance of the orchestra. Nearly all the desks for the second violins were occupied by ladies: beautiful young ladies. Personal beauty is not the strong point of West-end orchestras, and I thought the change an immense improvement until the performance began, when the fair fiddlers rambled from bar to bar with a certain sweet indecision that had a charm of its own, but was not exactly what Purcell and Handel meant. When I say that the performance began, I do not imply that it began punctually. The musicians began to drop in at about ten minutes past eight, and the audience were inclined to remonstrate; but an occasional apology from the conductor, Mr F. A. W. Docker, kept them in good humor.

Dido and Eneas is 200 years old, and not a bit the worse for wear. I daresay many of the Bowegians thought that the unintentional quaintnesses of the amateurs in the orchestra were Purcellian antiquities. If so, they were never more mistaken in their lives, Henry Purcell was a great composer: a very great composer indeed; and even this little boarding-school opera is full of his spirit, his freshness, his dramatic expression, and his

unapproached art of setting English speech to music. The
Handel Society did not do him full justice: the work, in fact, is
by no means easy; but the choir made up bravely for the distracting dances of the string quartet. Eneas should not have
called Dido Deedo, any more than Juliet should call Romeo
Ro-*may*-oh, or Othello call his wife Days-*day*-mona. If Purcell
chose to pronounce Dido English fashion, it is not for a Bow-
Bromley tenor to presume to correct him. Belinda, too, was
careless in the matter of time. She not only arrived after her part
had been half finished by volunteers from the choir, but in Oft
She Visits she lost her place somewhat conspicuously. An un-
named singer took Come away, fellow sailors, come away: that
salt sea air that makes you wonder how anyone has ever had the
face to compose another sailor's song after it. I quote the concluding lines, and wish I could quote the incomparably jolly
and humorous setting:

> Take a bowsy short leave of your nymphs on the shore;
>> And silence their mourning
>> With vows of returning,
> Though never intending to visit them more.

SAILORS (*greatly tickled*): Though never –!

OTHER SAILORS (*ready to burst with laughter*): Though
never –!

ALL (*uproariously*): Inte-en-ding to vi-isit them more.

I am sorry to have to add that the Handel choir, feeling that
they were nothing if not solemn, contrived to subdue this rous-
ing strain to the decorum of a Sunday school hymn; and it
missed fire accordingly. Of Alexander's Feast I need only say
that I enjoyed it thoroughly, even though I was sitting on a cane-
bottomed chair (Thackeray overrated this description of furniture) without adequate room for my knees. The band, reinforced
by wind and organ, got through with a healthy roughness that refreshed me; and the choruses were capital. Mr Bantock Pier-
point, the bass, covered himself with merited glory, and Mr John
Probert would have been satisfactory had he been more consist-
ently careful of his intonation. Miss Fresselle acquitted herself

fairly; but her singing is like that of the society generally: it lacks point and color. Mr Docker must cure his singers of the notion that choral singing is merely a habit caught in church, and that it is profane and indecorous to sing Handel's music as if it meant anything. That, however, is the worst I have to say of them. I am, on the whole, surprised and delighted with the East end, and shall soon venture there without my revolver. At the end of the concert, a gentleman, to my entire stupefaction, came forward and moved a vote of thanks to the performers. It was passed by acclamation, but without musical honors.

P.S. The Handel Society appeals urgently for tenors, a second bassoon, and horns. Surely every reader of The Star can at least play the second bassoon. Apply to Mr P. L. G. Webb, 3 Chandos Street, Cavendish Square, w.

Bayreuth: First Impressions

→⟶⟵←

1 August 1889

IMAGINE yourself in a state of high indignation at having paid a pound for admission to a theatre, and finding yourself in a dim freestone-colored auditorium, reminding you strongly of a lecture theatre by the steepness of the bank of seats and the absence of a gallery. But whereas most lecture theatres are fan-shaped or circular, with a rostrum at the pivot or centre, this one is wedge-shaped, with a shabby striped curtain cutting off the thin end of the wedge, the difference being that the parallel benches are straight instead of curved. Partition walls jut out at right angles to the wall of the building at intervals along the side, and break off short just in time to avoid getting between the people in the end seats and the stage. These walls which do not quite reach the ceiling, are surmounted by branches of lamps in round globes, which shed a dun-colored light over the dun-colored house. You come prepared by countless photographs and engravings for the shape of the place; but this prevailing dun tone, and the prevailing absence of cushion, curtain, fringe, gilding, or any gay theatrical garniture, with the steepness of the bank of seats (no pictures give you an adequate idea of this), make you inclined to think that the manager might really have touched up the place a little for you. But you have nothing else to complain of; for your hinged seat, though of uncushioned cane, is comfortably wide and broad, and your view of the striped curtain perfect. The highly esteemed ladies are requested by public notice obligingly their hats to remove, and those who have innocent little bonnets, which would not obstruct a child's view, carefully remove them. The ladies with the Eiffel hats, regarding them as objects of public interest, not second to any work of Wagner's, steadfastly disregard the notice; and Germany, with all its martinets, dare not enforce discipline. You open your libretto, your score, your synopsis of *leitmotifs*, or other idiotic device for distracting your attention from the performance; and immediately the lights go out and leave you in what for the moment seems all but total darkness. There is a clatter of cane seats turned down; a great rustle, as of wind through a forest, caused by 1300 skirts and coat tails coming into contact with the cane; followed by an angry hushing and hissing from overstrained Wagnerians who resent every noise by adding to it with an irritability much more trying to healthy nerves than the occasional inevitable dropping of a stick or opera-glass. Then the prelude is heard; and you at once recognize that you are in the most perfect theatre in the world for comfort, effect, and concentration of attention. You inwardly exclaim that you are hearing the prelude played for the first time as it ought to be played. And here, leaving you to enjoy yourself as a member of the analytical public, I strike in with the remark that the perfection is not in the performance, which does not touch the excellence of one which Richter conducted at the Albert Hall, but in the conditions of the performance. And I may say here, once for all, that the undiscriminating praise that is lavished on the Bayreuth representations is due to the effect of these conditions before the curtain and not behind it. The much boasted staging is marred by obsolete contrivances which would astonish us at the Lyceum as much as a return to candle-lighting or half price at nine o'clock. Mr Mansfield playing Richard III in the dress of Garrick, or Mr Irving Hamlet in that of Kemble, would seem modern and original compared with the unspeakable ballroom costume which Madame Materna dons to fascinate Parsifal in the second act. The magic flower garden would be simply the most horribly vulgar and foolish transformation scene ever allowed to escape from a provincial pantomime, were it not recommended to mercy by a certain enormous *naïveté* and a pleasantly childish love of magnified red blossoms and trailing creepers. As to the canvas set piece and Gower St sofa visibly pulled on to the stage with Madame Materna seductively reposing on it, the steam from a copper under the boards which filled the house with a smell of laundry and melted axillary guttapercha linings, the indescribable impossibility of the wigs and beards, the characterless historical-school draperies of the knights, the obvious wire connection of the electric light which glowed in the ruby bowl of the Holy Grail, and the senseless violation of Wagner's directions by allowing Gurnemanz and Parsifal to walk off the stage whilst the panoramic change of scene was taking place in the first act (obviously the absence of the two men who are supposed to be traversing the landscape reduces the exhibition to the alternative absurdities of the trees taking a walk or the auditorium turning round): all these faults shew the danger of allowing to any theatre, however imposing its associations, the ruinous privilege of exemption from vigilant and implacable criticism. The performance of Parsifal on Sunday last suffered additionally from Herr Grüning executing a hornpipe on the appearance of Klingsor with the sacred spear; but this was introduced not as an act of whimsical defiance, but under pressure of the desperate necessity of disentangling Parsifal's ankle from the snapped string on which the spear was presently to have flown at him.

Now if you, my Wagnerian friends, wonder how I can scoff thus at so impressive a celebration, I reply that Wagner is dead, and that the evil of deliberately making the Bayreuth Festival Playhouse a temple of dead traditions, instead of an arena for live impulses, has begun already. It is because I, too, am an enthusiastic Wagnerite that the Bayreuth management cannot deceive me by dressing itself in the skin of the dead lion. The life has not quite gone out of the thing yet: there are moments when the spirit of the master inspires the puppets, and the whole scene glows into real life. From the beginning of the Good Friday music in the last act, after the scene where the woman washes Parsifal's feet and dries them with her hair – the moment at which Parsifal's true character of Redeemer becomes unmistakeably obvious to the crassest Philistine globe-trotter present – the sacred fire descended, and the close of the representation was deeply impressive. Before that, a point had been brought out strongly here and there by individual artists; but nothing more. I shall return to the subject and deal more particularly with the two casts later on, when I see the work again on Thursday. For the present I need only warn readers that my censure of some of the scenic arrangements must not be allowed to obscure the fact that the Grail scene is unsurpassed as a stage picture; that the first scene, though conventional, is finely painted; and that the Spanish landscape, from which the magic garden suddenly withers (this is a capital effect), and the Good Friday landscape in the last act, are fine pieces of stage scenery.

Journey to Bayreuth

→>-<-

2 August 1889

I WRITE under difficulties this week. I am not a good sailor. After being rocked in the cradle of the deep all night, I am at present being rocked in a Dutch railway carriage. I have been in it for five hours, and I assure you that if an express were to come in the opposite direction on the same line of rails and smash the whole affair, Bassetto included, into pulp, I should make no unmanly complaints. After all, there is something grand in being able to look death in the face with a smile of welcome; but I should enjoy it more if I could look life in the face without feeling so poorly.

It is later in the day; and I think life is, perhaps, worth living after all. To drive up the Rhine from Bonn to Coblenz, whilst the hours advance from afternoon to night, is better than a dozen press views of different schools of landscape. Cologne Cathedral, too, has affected me. I am extremely susceptible to stained glass, and the old glass there transports me, whilst the new glass makes me long to transport it – with bricks. Yes, I confess I am enjoying the evening. I wish I were undressed and in bed, with twelve hours' sleep before me; I wish that when that terrific shower caught me in Cologne my mackintosh had not split up the back like a trick coat in a farce, throwing the younger posterity of the Three Kings into derisive convulsions. I wish I knew whether that very genial market woman really gave me, as she implied, an enormous bargain for the sake of my *beaux yeux* (one and eleven-pence for half a pound of grapes and six little hard pears), or whether she swindled me; and I wish I could go back by Channel Tunnel. But still, for the moment, I do not regret having been born.

Some hours have elapsed, and I now distinctly *do* regret having been born. Imagine reaching Würzburg at two in the morning, and being told to wait two and a half hours for a train to Bamberg. Imagine a wilderness of a German waiting-room – a place like a café running to seed for want of a little paint – crowded with people in various grades of wakefulness. The young what's-their-names wearing badges, and carrying military paraphernalia wrapped up in umbrella cases, are very wideawake indeed: they are continually breaking into Lorelei, or some other popular air, only to break out of it in quite British fashion the next moment. The men who are stretched on the two broad forms in the middle of the room, and on rows of chairs in the background, might be supposed asleep if a man could really sleep with the back of his neck pillowed on the handle of a travelling-bag, and his occiput taking an impression of the catch. The seated slumberers, with their arms folded on the table and their faces hidden upon them, are probably less miserable, especially those who are not at marble tables. I tried this plan for a moment myself; but it was a failure: after killing ten minutes by the familiar process of making them appear ten hours, I have taken to writing as the best way I know of making time seem too short (*ars longa, vita brevis*, you understand). The fearfully weary woman with the fretful child has just got up and tried a walk, after addressing to me a remark which I do not understand, but which I accept as a commission to see that nobody steals her luggage during her promenade.

Pshaw! describing a scene like this is like trying to draw one of the faces you see in a cloud. Already the noisy youngsters are gone, and the horizontal figures have transferred themselves, during their vertical intervals, to the trains which an official with a brutal bell and an undistinguished delivery enters to announce from time to time. There are but twelve of us now, including the two waiters, myself, and the child, who has, I am happy to say, left off worrying its mother to stare at the tremendous spectacle of Corno di Bassetto writing his sparkling Star column, and looking more melancholy and jaded over it than any infant's mind could have conceived. But hark! methinks I scent the morning air. The shunter's horn – a silly child's affair with a harmonium reed in it – takes a bustling tone as if it were paid so much a week to call the lark in time. A passing engine shews against the sky no longer as a bright gleaming mass of metal against a dead darkness, but as a black shadow on a dim grey galanty-sheet. And it is beginning to strike cold and raw! Ugh! What an idiot I was not to go on to Nuremberg; and what stupids they were to give me tickets via Bamberg! I feel that I shall slate something presently – Parsifal, probably.

After all, Bamberg has its merits. It was worth coming round to see: that affable young German gentleman at Cook's who sold me my tickets evidently knew a thing or two. How Bamberg manages to have so many rivers and bridges and yet to be on top of a group of hills I do not know: it is only another proof of the worthlessness of the commonplace that water will find its own level. The town has such an odd air of being built by persons with artistic instincts, but with the temperament which usually earns for its possessor the title of rum customer, that the climb up from the vegetable market, strong in marrows and carrots, under the Bridge House, decorated with frescoes exactly like the ones I used to produce on whitewashed walls with penny paints when I was a boy, and up to the Cathedral, freshened me more than all the naps I had snatched in the train from Würzburg: more even than the delightfully musical German of the two young ladies *en route* for Kissingen, who were my fellow-travellers to Schweinfurth. Really a perfect ante-Gothic cathedral of the plainest and most reasonable beauty, looking its best in the morning light.

Glancing through Baedeker as I bowl along Bayreuthwards I perceive that the chief feature of the Wagner district is a great lunatic asylum. At Neumarkt an official railway colporteur thrusts into my hand a great red placard inscribed with a WARNUNG! (German spelling is worse than indifferent) against pickpockets at Bayreuth. This is a nice outcome of Parsifal. In the town an enterprising tradesman offers 'the Parsifal slippers' at 2m. 50 the pair as 'the height of novelty'. It is a desperately stupid little town, this Bayreuth. I was never in Bath but once; and then they were trying to make it exciting by a meeting of the British Association which I addressed for a solid hour in spite of the secretary's urging me to be brief. Trying to make Bayreuth lively by a Wagner Festspiel is much the same thing.

However, there are hills with fine woods to wander through, and blackberries, raspberries, and other sorts of edible berries, about the names of which no two persons agree, to be had for the picking. On the top of the hill on which the theatre stands is a tower erected to the brave sons of Bayreuth who fell in 1870–71. Except that the tower is round, and that there is no courtly old lady to take toll and sell ginger-beer, you might, by a vigorous contraction of the imagination, fancy yourself on Leith Hill. The town contains a bust of Mr John Cobden Sanderson, with somebody else's name under it; also the most extravagantly and outrageously absurd fountain and equestrian statue in the world (of Margrave Somebody). Jean Paul Richter is much commemorated in the neighborhood. I am surprised to find how few faces I know here. Charles Dowdeswell, William Archer, Antoinette Sterling, Stavenhagen, Richter, Carl Armbruster, Pauline Cramer, Rimbault Dibdin, and Benjamin R.

Tucker of Boston, are all I can identify. It is desperately hard work, this daily scrutiny of the details of an elaborate performance from four to past ten. Yet there are people who imagine I am taking a holiday.

Tristan und Isolde

→-◄-◄

6 August 1889

TRISTAN AND ISOLDA comes off better than Parsifal by just so much as the impulse to play it is more genuine and the power to understand it more common. To enjoy Parsifal, either as a listener or an executant, one must be either a fanatic or a philosopher. To enjoy Tristan it is only necessary to have had one serious love affair; and though the number of persons possessing this qualification is popularly exaggerated, yet there are enough to keep the work alive and vigorous. In England it is not yet familiar: we contentedly lap dose after dose of such pap as the garden scene in Gounod's Faust, and think we are draining the cup of stage passion to the dregs. The truth is that all the merely romantic love scenes ever turned into music are pallid beside the second act of Tristan. It is an ocean of sentiment, immensely German, and yet universal in its appeal to human sympathy. At eight o'clock yesterday (Monday) I wondered that people fresh from such an experience did not rashly declare that all other music is leather and prunella; shrug their shoulders at the triviality of *La ci darem*; and denounce a proposal to try the effect of the fourth act of Les Huguenots as a direct incitement to crime.

The performance on Monday was an admirable one. After the scratch representations we are accustomed to in London, at which half the attention of the singers is given to the prompter, half to the conductor, and the rest to the character impersonated, the Bayreuth plays seem miracles of perfect preparedness. Nothing is forgotten; nothing is slurred; nothing on the stage contradicts its expression in the orchestra. At Covent Garden, where you cannot

47

get an artist even to open a letter or make a sword thrust within four bars of the chord by which the band expresses his surprise or his rage, the tithe of the thought and trouble taken here would work wonders. The orchestra, too, by certain methods of treating the instruments, produce many effects of which the tradition must be handed down orally; for most of them defy such directions as a composer can write into his score with any prospect of being rightly understood. Everything that can be done by educated men thoroughly in earnest is done: the shortcomings are those which only individual gifts can overcome.

That shortcomings did exist may be inferred from the fact that, except at those supreme moments at which the Wagnerian power sweeps everything before it, it is possible for an ungrateful visitor to feel heavily bored. The reason is that the singers, in spite of their formidable physique, thick powerful voices, and intelligent and energetic declamation, are not all interesting. They lack subtlety, grace, finesse, magnetism, versatility, delicacy of attack, freedom, individuality: in a word, genius. I remember how Carl Hill sang the part of Mark when I first heard that second act: how we were made to understand the simple dignity, the quiet feeling, the noble restraint, the subdued but penetrating reproach of the old king's address to the hero whom he had loved as a son, and in whose arms he surprises his virgin wife. Herr Betz gave us hardly any of this. He turned his head away, and lifted his hands, and sang most dolefully: nobody was sorry when he had said his say and was done with it. Only a few months ago, at the Portman Rooms, I heard Mr Grove, who makes no pretension to the eminence of Herr Betz, sing this scene with much truer expression. But when Hill sang the part Wagner was conducting; so perhaps the comparison is hardly fair to Betz. In the third act again Vogl surpassed Charles II in point of being an unconscionably long time dying. Wagner's heroes have so much to say that if they have not several ways of saying it (Vogl has exactly two – a sentimental way and a vehement way) the audience is apt to get into that temper which, at English public meetings, finds vent in cries of 'Time!' For the fuller a poem is, the duller is an empty recitation of it.

The honors of the occasion were carried off by the women. The men shewed that they had been heavily drilled and were under orders; but Frau Sucher and Fraülein Staudigl played as if the initiative were their own. Frau Sucher, indeed, is not a good subject for leading-strings. Her Isolda is self-assertive and even explosive from beginning to end: impetuous in love, violent in remorse, strong in despair. Frau Sucher has the singer's instinct in a degree exceptionally keen for Bayreuth: she, like Frau Materna, can fall back sometimes on methods of expression solely musical. Fraülein Staudigl's Brangaena was excellent. If I were asked to point to the page of music in which the most perfect purity of tone would produce the greatest effect I think I should select the warning of Brangaena from the tower top to the lovers in the garden. I cannot say that Fraülein Staudigl quite satisfied me in this indescribable episode; but I can praise her warmly for not having fallen much further short of perfection than she actually did. The orchestra, conducted by Felix Mottl, played with an absolute precision and a touch of austerity which reminded me of Costa, who, obsolete as his tastes were, and quickly as he has been forgotten, deserves this reminiscence for having kept his foot down so long on slovenly and vulgar orchestral work. So much so that I sometimes wish he were alive again; though there was a time when – musically speaking, you understand – I heartily wished him dead. Curious, that Tristan and Isolda in Bayreuth should have set me talking about Costa, of all men that ever were!

Perhaps the reason why these Bayreuth artists interest me so much less than they ought to, is that they make no mistakes, and I am consequently deprived of an irritant to which I have become accustomed in London. Whatever it is, I sighed more than once for ten minutes of Covent Garden. Not, of course, for the Covent Garden orchestra, or the conductor, or the cuts, or the stalls and boxes, or the late hours, or the superficialities, or the general cloudiness as to the meaning of the stage business, or the pointless Italian verse. But I could have borne a stave or two from Jean de Reszke and Lassalle with a tranquil mind. It is true that Herr Gudehus understands the part of Walther much better than

De Reszke: he acts with humor and intelligence, and sings by no means without fervor and power. Moreover, he is venerable; whereas our Polish favorite is a mere sprig of forty or thereabouts. Again, Reichmann gives a more characteristic portrait of the cobbler master-singer of Nuremberg than Lassalle: one, too, much fuller of suggestive detail. And though his voice is much the worse for wear, there is, here and there in his compass, still a rich note or two; and he was able to finish the part bravely, though the last hundred bars or so evidently cost him a severe effort. But in musical charm neither Gudehus nor Reichmann touched De Reszke and Lassalle, though at every other point they far surpassed them. I wish some man of science would provide critics with a psychology capable of explaining how the same man may sing through an opera like a genius and act through it like a country gentleman; or conversely, why he may interpret the book like a student and philosopher, and sing through the score like an improved foghorn. The first case prevails in London and makes Covent Garden frivolous: the other monopolizes Bayreuth and makes the Festival Plays heavy. The performance was an arduous one, the third act lasting two hours. Richter conducted; and this is as good a place as another to say that he is by far the freest, strongest, and most gifted conductor of the three, though he left Parsifal to Levi (it is an open secret that Wagner at first offered the work to the Gentile conductor), and does not always take the trouble to secure the faultless precision attained by Mottl in Tristan. I have heard nothing played here with such an effect as the prelude to the third act; and the judgment, the good husbandry, and – at the right moment – the massive force with which Richter got the maximum of effect in the scenes of crowd and tumult were great feats of generalship. The stage management was above praise: how much it did to make the situations intelligible could only be adequately felt by those who had seen Die Meistersinger in theatres where nothing but a few of the simpler incidents seem to be thoroughly understood by anybody concerned. The final scene was one of the most imposing I have ever seen on the stage; and here, as in the previous acts, the effect produced was not the result of money freely lavished, but of care conscientiously taken. The waltz was charming because it was a dance and not a ballet (I wish I could persuade Stewart Headlam that ballet is the death of dancing). Anyhow, the scene at Bayreuth was no more like that at Covent Garden than a picture by Teniers is like an *aquarelle* by Dubufe. Of the principal artists, besides those of whom I have already spoken, the most distinguished was Friedrichs, who played Beckmesser like a finished comedian. Frau Staudigl again shewed considerable intelligence as an actress in the part of Magdalena; and Fraülein Dressler's Eva was a good Eva as Evas go, though she crowned Walther at the end with an appallingly flat imitation shake. Hofmüller was comparatively bright as David. The remarkable completeness and depth of the impression produced shewed the wisdom of performing great works without mutilation, at whatever tax on the time and endurance of the audience. The flood of melody throughout the work astonished the few survivors of the sceptics who originated the brilliant theory that Wagner devoted his existence to avoiding anything of a musical nature in his compositions.

The place is by this time full of English. I shall retreat to Nuremberg after Parsifal.

Parsifal

7 August 1889

THIS Parsifal is a wonderful experience: not a doubt of it. The impression it makes is quite independent of liking the music or understanding the poem. Hardly anybody has the slightest idea of what it all means; many people are severely fatigued by it; and there must be at least some who retain enough of the old habit of regarding the theatre as an exception to the doctrine of Omnipresence, to feel some qualms concerning the propriety of an elaborate make-believe of Holy Communion, culminating in the descent of a stuffed dove through a flood of electric radiance. Yet Parsifal is the magnet that draws people to Bayreuth and disturbs their journey thence with sudden fits of desperate desire to go back again. When you leave the theatre after your first Parsifal you may not be conscious of having brought away more than a phrase or two of *leitmotif* mingled with your burden of weariness and disappointment. Yet before long the music begins to stir within you and haunt you with a growing urgency that in a few days makes another hearing seem a necessity of life. By that time, too, you will have been converted to the Church and Stage Guilds' view that the theatre is as holy a place as the church and the function of the actor no less sacred than that of the priest.

The second performance given during my stay at Bayreuth was much better than the first. It is sometimes difficult for a critic to feel sure that an improvement of this sort is not in his own temper rather than in what he is listening to; but as I found Klingsor decidedly worse than before and was conscious of one or two points at which Fräulein Malten as Kundry fell short of Frau Materna, the difference must have been objective, since, had it been merely subjective, the apparent changes would all have been, like my mood, from worse to better. Malten has several advantages over Materna in playing Kundry. Not only is she passably slim, but her long thin lips and finely-turned chin, with her wild eyes, give her a certain air of *beauté de diable*. Only an air, it is true, but enough for a willing audience. Her voice, though a little worn, is bright; and her delivery is swift and telling. Altogether, one may say that her individuality, though it would not startle London, is quite magnetic in Bayreuth. Frau Materna, the rival Kundry, is not perceptibly lighter than she was when she sang at the Albert Hall in 1877. She is comely, but matronly. Still, as Kundry is as old as the hills no complaint need be made on this score; indeed, the part is one which a very young woman would play worse than a mature one, unless she were a young woman of extraordinary genius and precocity. At moments Materna's singing is grand, and her acting powerful: at other moments she holds up the corner of an absurd scarf as if it had descended to her from a provincial Mrs Siddons. Fräulein Malten also clings to a scarf rather more than is good for the sobriety of spectators with an untimely sense of fun. But nobody laughs. It is a point of honor not to laugh in the Wagner Theatre, where the chances offered to ribalds are innumerable: take as instances the solemn death and funeral of the stuffed swan; the letting out of Parsifal's tucks when his mailed shirt is taken off and his white robe pulled down; and the vagaries of the sacred spear, which either refuses to fly at Parsifal at all or else wraps its fixings round his ankles like an unnaturally thin boa constrictor. Nevertheless, nobody behaves otherwise than they would in church. The performance is regarded on all hands as a rite. Miss Pauline Cramer, if she had no deeper feeling than a desire to oblige the management, like Montariol at Covent Garden, would hardly have volunteered for the silent part of the youth whose whole duty it is to uncover the Grail. As to Frau Materna, it is impossible to believe that when she goes up nearly the whole depth of the Grail scene on her knees, she is only aiming at a stage effect. As such, it is not worth the physical exertion it costs. Van Dyck, though not so steady a singer as Grüning, has a certain impulsive *naïveté* which, with his engaging physical exuberance, makes him the better Parsifal. The part is a unique one, full of never-to-be-forgotten situations. Impressive as his first Grail scene is, nine-tenths of its effect would be lost without the 'innocent fool' gazing dumbly at it in the corner, only to be bustled out as a goose when it is over. His appearance on the rampart of Klingsor's castle, looking down in wonder at the flower maidens in the enchanted garden, is also a memorable point. And that long kiss of Kundry's from which he learns so much is one of those pregnant simplicities which stare the world in the face for centuries and yet are never pointed out except by great men.

Concert at Her Majesty's

24 August 1889

THE managers at Her Majesty's kindly sent me a ticket for Thursday night to hear a young lady of nine play the violin. I prefer not to be an accomplice in the exploitation of young ladies of nine, so I did not go until the following night, when classical doings were afoot. Signor Bevignani's orchestra has settled down into the most charming drawing-room orchestra conceivable at a promenade concert. It has no force; but it is polite and delicate, and can put in the touches for wood wind and horns into a Mendelssohn symphony or a Mozart accompaniment with the gentlest of breaths. It was, of course, not within ten tons of the weight of the Zauberflöte overture; but not at Bayreuth itself was the Meistersinger prize song more sweetly accompanied. M. de Pachmann also played very prettily. The whole atmosphere was pre-Wagner, reminding one of Mendelssohn and Spohr and the Prince Consort. Also, perhaps, of Poole and Lincoln and Bennett. I was glad, for the honor of a once famous name, when Miss Marie Tietjens, whom I had not heard before, sang *Vedrai carino* quite unexceptionally, with a voice still fragile, and hardly quite formed yet in the middle, but of remarkably pure and pleasant tone and perfect intonation. To Mr Holman Black, who attempted the serenade from Don Giovanni, and came off rather nervously, I will just say that he has learnt the song from an edition in which the words are wrongly set, a very easy thing to do; for none of the English editions, as far as I know, except Novello's, contain the restorations of Mozart's phrasing to be found in Breitkopf and Hartel's great edition. The lines *'Tu che il zucchero porte in mezzo core'*, are now really out of the question as Mr Black sings them. He will find, too, that the effect of the last bar of the song is not in the B, C, D which he makes so much of, but in the lower D. Fashionable baritones can make nothing of the song, because they sacrifice the middle of their voice to the top. When a composer uses the contrast between the upper and lower D – one of the most effective of vocal contrasts with a completely cultivated bass voice – they are at a loss. However, it is better to fail on the low note written by Mozart than to try for a high F sharp, as the fashion once was. Mr Black afterwards rashly sang a new setting of The Minstrel Boy by somebody bearing the illustrious name of Shelley. The audience took this rather in bad part, not unjustifiably; for the new tune was a commonplace march, much inferior to the old one. On the other hand, they encored Mr Lloyd rapturously in the Preislied from Die Meistersinger and in Alice, where art thou? and behaved handsomely to M. Tivadar Nachez, who fiddled, and to Mr Howard Reynolds. Among the announcements for this evening is 'Mrs Shaw, the American Lady Whistler'. I cannot make this out: if she is Mrs Shaw, how can she be Lady Whistler? Senor Albeniz takes the place of Mr de Pachmann as solo pianist.

Mendelssohn

→►-◄←

22 November 1889

OF all the thousands of Star readers who have delighted in Mendelssohn and loved him only one has cared enough to hurl a postcard at me for what I said about St Paul. Here it is.

'AN IGNORANT SELF-CONCEITED ASS is the Star musical critic (!) who scribbles on Mendelssohn and the Oratorio of St Paul at the Crystal Palace on Saturday!!!

'He should be put under a glass case and exhibited at Barnum's menagerie; for SURELY he has the LONGEST PAIR OF EARS IN ALL LONDON.

'The animal!

'Who was his father? – and who his mother? The breed should be perpetuated as a curiosity!!!'

My heart warms to this anonymous correspondent. The postcard is an outburst of genuine feeling about music, somewhat unsocially expressed, perhaps, but still heartfelt. Yet I shall probably often again wound that feeling, because, for the musical critic in England, Mendelssohn is The Enemy. Until we have got far enough to recoil from Elijah flippantly rattling off his atrocious 'God is angry with the wicked every day' we shall never fathom the depths of truly great music. Mendelssohn, who was shocked at Auber's writing an opera in which a girl sang *Oui c'est demain* (meaning 'Tomorrow I shall be a bride') at her looking-glass before going to bed, was himself ready to serve up the chopping to pieces of the prophets of the grove with his richest musical spice to suit the compound of sanctimonious cruelty and base materialism which his patrons, the British Pharisees, called their religion. If my correspondent will compare such work as his with Parsifal, and his career with that of the man who produced Parsifal, he (or she; for the handwriting is of uncertain sex) will understand why Wagner once said, speaking of an occasion when Mendelssohn invited him to applaud an orchestral full gallop through the beautiful slow trio of Beethoven's eighth symphony, 'I thought I saw before me an abyss of superficiality.' The Philharmonic orchestra scampers through its work in the same elegantly superficial manner to this day, thanks to Mendelssohn. Probably all my correspondent really means is that Mendelssohn composed music of exquisite grace and tenderness. I am no more insensible to that than was Wagner, who used to ask his pianist friends to play Mendelssohn's overtures for him. But when I am asked to spend an afternoon listening to oratorios that must stand or fall, not by the grace or tenderness of their prettiest strains, but by the depth and moral dignity of their conception, then Mendelssohn gets roughly handled; and it serves him abundantly right. . . .

High Society

›+‹

6 December 1889

I REMEMBER once coming to loggerheads with the late Dr Francis Hueffer, about fifteen seconds after the opening of our first conversation, on the subject of musical culture in English society. Whenever the subject arose between us, I declared that English society did not care about music – did not know good music from bad. He replied, with great force, that I knew nothing about it; that nobody had ever seen me in really decent society; that I moved amidst cranks, Bohemians, unbelievers, agitators, and – generally speaking – riff-raff of all sorts; and that I was merely theorising emptily about the people whom I called bloated aristocrats. He described, by way of example, an evening at Lord Derby's house, where he had greatly enjoyed some excellent music; and he asked me whether I knew that such music was, in a quiet way, a constant grace of the best sort of English social life. I suggested that he should give me an opportunity to judge for myself by introducing me to these circles; but this he entirely declined to do; having no confidence whatever in my power of behaving myself in a seemly manner for five consecutive minutes.

On the first occasion it so happened, fortunately for me, that a firm of music publishers, having resolved to venture on the desperate step of publishing six new pianoforte sonatas, had just sent out a circular containing an appeal *ad misericordiam* that at least a few people would, either in public spirit or charity, take the unprecedented step of buying these compositions. I promptly hurled this at Hueffer's head, and asked whether that looked like evidence of a constant and enlightened patronage such as the upper classes accord to racing, millinery, confectionery, and in a minor degree to literature and painting (for, hang it all! even if the sonatas were not as good as Beethoven's, they were at any rate no duller than the average three-volume novel or Academy picture). There the subject dropped, my method of controversy being at that time crudely unscrupulous and extravagant. Heuffer, I fancy, regarded me as an unschooled dangerous character; but once, when I was perched on the gunwale of a wagon in Hyde Park, filling up some ten minutes of a 'demonstration' with the insufferable oratorizing which is the only sort feasible on such occasions, I was astonished to see his long golden beard and massive brow well to the front among the millions of 'friends and fellow citizens'. He never told me what he thought about the contrast between the new musical criticism demonstrating on wagons in the sunlight, and the old, groping in perpetual evening dress from St James's Hall to Covent Garden Opera House and back again.

One point I might have put to him, but didn't, is that when you get up a musical entertainment for the exclusive delectation of the nobs, you must either be content with a very scanty audience, in which case the nobs will not think it good enough to come again, or else pack the room with a contingent of musical deadheads, who are not nobs, nor even respectable Philistine snobs, but rank outsiders – though you would be surprised at the costly entertainments, operatic and otherwise, that are run solely for their sake, and that of the jaded pressmen. Last Friday, happening to have an invitation from the Grosvenor Club to their 'ladies' night' at the Grosvenor Gallery, I thought I would go and see whether things were altering at all. For the Grosvenor Club, you must know, is no vulgar free-and-easy; and its concerts, from 9.30 to midnight, are never wholly nobless.

On entering that Bond Street portal which was brought here bodily all the way from Italy, and approaching the stairs which I have so often worn with the weary feet of an art critic, I found on one side a descending stream of sad and hollow people, and on the other an ascending one, flushed and swollen. By this I perceived that the refreshments were downstairs; and I hurried up with all convenient speed. Here I found a nob or two, a dead-head or two, and a vast majority of solid snobs. No celebrities, no literary lot, no journalistic lot, no artistic lot, no Bohemian lot, nothing (to speak of) except plain snobbery, more or less choice. In short, there were – professionally engaged musicians excepted – not above twelve people in the room known to me; and I should have congratulated Mr Prange on such an entirely satisfactory result if I had been quite certain that he would have appreciated the full force of this final proof of the respectability of the gathering, and of the success of his elimination of the great army of 'private view' people.

I could not get a program; and when Signor Ducci went to the piano, and Mr Radcliffe took his flute, Mr Mann his horn, and the fiddlers four their fiddles, I wondered what was coming. It proved to be resurrection pie of the dustiest flavor. For a long time I was at a loss. I thought vaguely of Clementi, of Dussek, of Field, of all the Sir Arthur Sullivans that existed before Mendelssohn's time. Not until several elegantly empty movements had worn themselves out did I hit on the right man: on Hummel, the genteel, the talented, the tastefully barren. Here are serenades by

Mozart, chamber music with wind parts by Schubert, by Weber, by Schumann, by Mendelssohn, by Brahms, all ready to Signor Ducci's hand; and he goes and digs up Jean Nepomuk Hummel! One unfortunate gentleman said to me: 'These things are very nice, of course; but they are very long.' Forgetting that I was for once among respectable people, I morosely expressed an opinion that this particular thing was strongly qualified rubbish. 'Oh' said he 'you are so very critical: I daresay it does not come up to *your* standard. But it was certainly too long for a place like this.' Thus does music get into disrepute. If my friend had heard Beethoven's septet, he would have been delighted. Hearing Hummel instead, he concluded that it was in the nature of classical music to be dull; and he will probably think so to his dying day.

However, the choicer spirits sat in the front of the room and faithfully listened. The others sat at the back and talked. How they talked! One young lady, who must, I should think, be the champion chatterbox of the universe, so outdid with her tongue the most rapid flights of Signor Ducci's fingers that I stole round three times through the east gallery merely to see whether she had stopped from exhaustion; but she was as fresh as an aviary each time. Another lady, who coaches me in the ways of good society, and makes certain prearranged warning signals to me when I eat with my knife or help myself to potatoes with my fingers, was very severe with me because I took sides with the front of the room and listened to the unimpeachable Jean Nepomuk. 'You were a failure there,' she said next day. 'Everybody was noticing your disgraceful behaviour. You will never be a gentleman.' 'What should I have done?' I demanded. 'I say nothing' she replied, 'about your not bringing us down to the refreshment room, and your furtively leaving before you had seen us off in a cab. But you should at least have come and *talked* to us.' 'But that would have disturbed the music' I pleaded. 'Music!' she retorted, with scorn. 'The Grosvenor is a private club where some rather crack people go: not a concert room. People go there to talk. Besides, you *scowled*.' On reflection, I daresay I did. I would suggest to Mr Prange that in future a curtain should shut off the east gallery from the west, and that the fireman should be employed to keep the musical section and the loquacious section in different rooms.

Visit to Paris

>-<

11 April 1890

I AM strongly of opinion that the Channel Tunnel should be proceeded with at once. There are worse things than foreign invasions, worse things even than foreign conquests, worse things than the extinction of England as a nation, if you come to that. I came over yesterday morning from Calais; and – but enough! The subject is not dignified; and it is hackneyed. All I will say is, that never again whilst I live – and yet I have made the same vow before, and broken it. Still, do not suppose that that silver streak of which you are so proud does not cost you something in the way of Continental musical news in the course of the year. But for it, The Star would be as great a musical power in Europe as it is in England.

Paris is, as usual, imposing on American greenhorns and British Philistines as a city artistic before everything, with specialities in cookery and well-dressed women. I am not an artistic novice, English or American; and I am not to be taken in. Paris is what it has always been: a pedant-ridden failure in everything that it pretends to lead. Mozart found it so more than a hundred years ago. Wagner found it so half a century ago: Corno di Bassetto regrets to say that he finds it so today. In music, it prides itself on its Opera, which is about twenty years behind Covent Garden; and Covent Garden, as everybody knows, is thirty years behind time: even New York leaving it nowhere. I went to the Paris Opera on Monday to fulfil my mission of hearing Saint-Saëns' new opera Ascanio. I need not waste many words on the music of it. There is not an original phrase in it from beginning to end. The tragic scenes are secondhand Verdi; the love scenes are secondhand Gounod; the 'historic' scenes are secondhand Meyerbeer. A duller potboiler I would not desire to hear anywhere. The orchestra is hardly better than the Covent Garden orchestra was in the seventies, before we got tired of the Gye-Mapleson managements that learned nothing and forgot nothing, and passed Vianesi, the conductor, on to Paris, where his immense industry, his cleverness, his ostentation, and his thorough superficiality enabled him to take root at once. Vianesi looks younger than ever, and is still on the alert for opportunities of turning conspicuously to the wood wind and brass, and offering them superfluous leads to shew how completely he has the score at his finger-ends; whilst the men have cultivated his slapdash, noisy style – or want of style – to the highest imperfection.

As to the singers, there is Lassalle, who brings down the house in a roaring duet with the tenor in the second act, and moves it to sentimental admiration in a mock pathetic passage in the fourth, beginning, 'Enfants: je ne vous en veux pas.' Lassalle can hardly believe in the part of Benvenuto Cellini; but he believes immensely in Lassalle, and so manages to make things go with an effective air of conviction. Madame Adiny is undeniably what we call a fine figure of a woman; but her tremolo and her superb screaming power leave in the shade even the lady who played Desdemona here in Verdi's Otello at the Lyceum last year. Plançon, as Francis I, and Madame Eames, as Colombe, sang pleasantly enough; and I have no right to find fault with Madame Bosman as a capable if not highly distinguished representative of the old-fashioned type of 'dramatic' singer, merely because I object to the entire species. The acting was the old impossible Richardson's Show strutting and swaggering, pitiful to see; and the libretto, like the music, was a string of commonplaces, culminating in Madame Adiny keeping Madame Bosman in a golden shrine in a public room for three days, at the expiry of which Madame Bosman was found dead 'for Benvenuto's sake,' which was the more affecting inasmuch as there was not the smallest reason why she should have got into the shrine in the first place or forborne to call on somebody to let her out in the second.

On the whole, I am afraid I must dismiss Ascanio as an

elaborate and expensive tomfoolery, and applaud the wisdom of those frequenters who came only for the ballet, which, though artificial as it well could be – classical, in short – was good of its kind. Yet Ascanio bored me less than Barbier's Joan of Arc at the Porte St Martin, with Gounod's music, and Sarah Bernhardt in the title part. Barbier, as everybody knows, is the man to go to if you want a great subject debased for operatic purposes. He can turn a masterpiece by Shakespear or Goethe into a trashy melodrama in the twinkling of an eye. He fell on Joan of Arc years ago and fixed her up (no other expression conveys the process) for the Gaieté. Now she is dragged to light again with considerable excisions – all heartily welcome – for Madame Bernhardt. In the music, Gounod imitates himself almost as mechanically as Saint-Saëns, and more exclusively. The best number is the vision of St Margaret and St Catherine. Even now, when his fount runs yet drier than in the last decade, Gounod can always write heavenly music. But Sarah is really too bad. We all know her way of pretending to act when there is no part for her – how sweetly she intones her lines and poses like a saint. This is what she does in Joan. There is no acting because there is no play; but she sends the lines out in a plaintive stream of melody throughout which only a fine ear can catch the false ring. You would almost swear that they meant something and that she was in earnest. Not until the final scene at the stake does the affair become thin enough for even the American and British tripper to see through it. Sarah did not wink once: perhaps because she did not catch my eye, perhaps because she was in no humor for making fun of herself. It must be wearisome to keep up that make-believe night after night, knowing all the time that her serious work is going on without her at the Français.

Of course, I went to the Français for the sake of the traditions of the house of Molière, and found them to consist of equal parts of gag and horseplay, in no way superior – distinctly the contrary, in fact – to those established only the other day in Mr Benson's company for Hamlet and The Taming of the Shrew. But if the traditions are feeble, the acting is not; and not many things are more enjoyable than an Easter Monday afternoon performance of Le Bourgeois Gentilhomme by the Comédie Française. Monsieur Jourdain can only be enjoyed in Paris, because he is himself bourgeois Paris incarnate. When the play is over you can continue your study of his flunkeyism in his petrified Lord-Mayor's-coach of an opera house; his helpless incapacity for art, and consequent subjection to any pedant who will talk to him about something that he can understand (something quite beside the purpose of art, necessarily) in the Louvre; and his petty rationalism and delight in unreasonable scraps of logic anywhere you please. If I ever take to playwriting (one never knows how low one may fall) I shall do a London Bourgeois Gentilhomme – quite as curious a creature in his way.

However, my main business here is not with the Comédie Française, but with a certain 'Soirée Musicale et Littéraire du Vendredi Saint' at the Winter Circus. The sensation here was the appearance of the divine Sarah in a divine character – that of the Virgin Mary, no less. She did more than this, however: she doubled her part with that of Mary Magdalen. Philippe Garnier confined himself to the leading character of Jesus; and Brémont compendiously undertook Pilate, Annas, Caiaphas, Peter, and Judas Iscariot. The work was described as 'a mystery in five parts' by Edmond Haraucourt, and was entitled The Passion. A large dose of Berlioz, Beethoven, and Wagner was administered first to get us into the proper frame of mind; and then the mystery began. Sarah, in a dress of the purest, softest white, and with her complexion made up with really exquisite delicacy into a faint blush that could hardly have been more virginal, was well received. The Passion began amid a hush of expectation, and soon proved to be fully equal in depth of thought and novelty of illustration to our finest specimens of modern oratorio libretti. Sarah sang – sung as usual, holding the book in her right hand and waving her left in the air with a rhythmic persuasiveness that did wonders in soothing the distressing cough that soon became epidemic. On the whole the audience bore up bravely until Garnier rose to deliver a sort of Sermon on the Mount some forty minutes long. In quarter of an hour or so the coughing took a new tone: it became evident that the more impatient spirits were beginning to cough on purpose, though their lungs were as sound as Garnier's own. Then came a voice crying 'Music, music,' followed by applause, laughter, and some faint protest. Garnier went on, as if deaf. Presently another voice, in heartfelt appeal, cried, 'Enough, enough.' The reception of this was unmistakably sympathetic; and Sarah's shoulders gathered themselves expressively; but Garnier held on like grim death; and again the audience held their hand for a moment on the chance of his presently stopping; for it seemed impossible that he could go on much longer. But he did; and the storm broke at last all the more furiously because it had been so long pent up. In the midst of it a gentleman rushed down the grades of the amphitheatre; crossed the arena; and shook hands demonstratively with Sarah, then Garnier, then with Brémont. This was Haraucourt himself; and he capped his protest by shaking his fist at the audience, who reiterated their fundamental disagreement with him on the merits of his poem by yells of disapproval. Hereupon, exasperated beyond endurance, he took the extreme step of informing them that if they persisted in their behavior he would there and then leave the room. The threat prevailed. An awestruck silence fell upon the multitude: and the poet was moving loftily towards his seat when a lady, presumably his wife, threw herself on his neck and rained kisses on him. This affecting spectacle moved the gentlemen in the neighborhood to offer him their hands, which he took in an impressive attitude. Then he sat down; and the imperturbable Garnier started again. But soon the conviction spread that even at the risk of Haraucourt fulfilling his terrible threat, the speech must be stopped. Garnier, whose demeanor throughout was a model of perfect taste, at last exchanged glances with his colleagues, and then with the politest deprecation began: 'Ladies and gentlemen: if you dont wish it' – whereupon the people in the arena expressed their opinion that the conduct of the five franc snobs was disgraceful, and the snobs in question vehemently gave Garnier to understand that there was no 'if' at all in the question – that they didnt wish it and wouldnt have it. Sarah, in lively pantomime, conveyed her thanks to the arena; but I could not help suspecting that she was privately of the gallery's opinon. At last the three artists held a consultation, at the end of which Garnier sat down, and Sarah started at a scene only a few pages from the end. The audience accepted the compromise; Haraucourt made no further protest except by applauding occasionally; and the remainder of The Passion was dispatched without further interruption.

The anti-Wagner party was present in full force. It consists of six old gentlemen, more or less like the Duke of Cambridge in personal appearance, who make faces and stop their ears whenever an unprepared major ninth occurs in the harmony. As the audience was some thousands strong, and enthusiastically opposed to the veterans, they did not make much headway. Wagner always maintained that the great Tannhäuser fiasco was a success with the gallery; and there is no serious reason to doubt that he was right. Lamoureux's orchestra played with refinement and precision; but the first movement of the C minor symphony was taken in the old empty, hurried, vapidly elegant way; and in the overture to Tannhäuser the brass, reinforced by two extra cornets and a fourth trombone (a monstrous license), played like a coarse cavalry band, and blared out the Pilgrims' March in a most detestable manner, making the famous violin figure quite inaudible. One moral of which is that London, which declined to accept Lamoureux as a great conductor, and took Richter to its bosom, is as far ahead of Paris in musical judgment as in most other things.

MUSIC IN LONDON
1890–94

Don Giovanni

>+>+<

13 May 1891

EVER since I was a boy I have been in search of a satisfactory performance of Don Giovanni; and I have at last come to see that Mozart's turn will hardly be in my time. I have had no lack of opportunities and disappointments; for the Don is never left long on the shelf, since it is so far unlike the masterpieces of Wagner, Berlioz, and Bach, that it cannot be done at all without arduous preparation. Any opera singer can pick up the notes and tumble through the concerted pieces with one eye on the conductor: any band can scrape through the orchestral parts at sight. Last year and the year before, it was tried in this fashion for a night at Covent Garden, with D'Andrade as Don Juan, and anybody who came handy in the other parts. This year it has been recognized that trifling with Mozart can be carried too far even for the credit of the Royal Italian Opera.

At the performance last Thursday, the first three acts of the four (twice too many) into which the work is divided at Covent Garden shewed signs of rehearsal. Even the last had not been altogether neglected. In the orchestra especially the improvement was marked. Not that anything very wonderful was accomplished in this department: the vigorous passages were handled in the usual timid, conventional way; and the statue music, still as impressive as it was before Wagner and Berlioz were born, was muddled through like a vote of thanks at the end of a very belated public meeting. But the overture was at least attentively played; and in some of the quieter and simpler numbers the exhalations of the magical atmosphere of the Mozartian orchestra were much less scanty and foggy than last year, when I could not, without risk of being laughed at, have assured a novice that in the subtleties of dramatic instrumentation Mozart was the greatest master of them all. The cast was neither a very bad nor a very good one. Its weakest point was the Leporello of Isnardon.

Lacking the necessary weight in the middle of his voice, as well as the personal force demanded by the character, he was quite unable to lead the final section of the great sextet, Mille torbidi pensieri, which, thus deprived of its stage significance, became a rather senseless piece of 'absolute music'. Again, in O statua gentilissima, he hardly seized a point from beginning to end.

Now if an artist has neither voice enough nor musical perception enough to interpret forcibly and intelligently such an obvious and simple dramatic transition as that which follows the incident of the statue nodding acceptance of the invitation to supper, he is not fit to meddle with Mozart. Isnardon certainly makes a considerable show of acting throughout the opera; but as he is only trying to be facetious – abstractly facetious, if I may say so – without the slightest feeling for his part, the effect is irritating and irrelevant. Such pieces of business as his pointing the words, Voi sapete quel che fa, by nudging Elvira with his elbow at the end of Madamina, almost make one's blood boil. Poor old Sganarelle-Leporelle, with all his failings, was no Yellow-plush: he would not have presumed upon a familiarity of that character with Donna Elvira, even if she had been a much meeker and less distinguished person than Molière made her. There is one man in Mr Harris's company whose clear artistic duty it is to play Leporello; and he, unfortunately, is an arrant *fainéant*, whose identity I charitably hide under the designation of Brother Edouard, which, I need hardly add, is not that under which he appears in the bills. In Leporello he would have one of the greatest parts ever written, exactly suited to his range, and full of points which his musical intelligence would seize instinctively without unaccustomed mental exertion. And now that I have begun sketching a new cast, I may as well complete it. Dalla sua pace is not an easy song to sing; but if Jean de Reszke were to do it justice, the memory thereof would abide when all his Gounod successes were lapsed and lost.

With Giulia Ravogli as Zerlina, and the rest of the parts allotted much as at present, a tremendous house would be drawn. Nevertheless the tremendous house would be bored and kept late for its trains unless the representation were brought up to date by the following measures. Take a pot of paste, a scissors and some tissue paper, and start on the *recitativo secco* by entirely expunging the first two dialogues after the duel and before Ah, chi mi dice mai. Reduce all the rest to such sentences as are barely necessary to preserve the continuity of the action. Play the opera in two acts only. And use the time thus gained to restore not only the Don's song, Metà di voi, which Faure used to sing, but, above all, the last three movements of the second finale, thereby putting an end for ever to the sensational vulgarity of bringing down the curtain on the red fire and the ghost and the trapdoor. There are other suppressed pages of the score to be reconsidered – a capital song which gets Leporello off the stage after the sextet, a curiously old-fashioned tragic air, almost Handelian, for Elvira between Là ci darem and the quartet, and a comic duet for Zerlina and Leporello, one of the later Vienna interpolations, which, however, is a very dispensable piece of buffoonery.

To return to the actual Don Giovanni of Thursday last, I need say no more of Miss de Lussan, who does not grow more interesting as her voice loses freshness and sustaining power and her manner becomes perter and trickier, than that she is one of those Zerlinas who end Batti, batti, on the upper octave of the note written, as a sort of apology for having been unable to do anything else with the song. The effect of this suburban grace can be realized by anyone who will take the trouble to whistle Pop goes the Weasel with the last note displaced an octave.

I am sorry to add that alterations of Mozart's text were the order of the evening, every one of the singers lacking Mozart's exquisite sense of form and artistic dignity. Maurel, though he stopped short of reviving the traditional atrocity of going up to F sharp in the serenade, did worse things by dragging an F natural into the end of Finch' han del vino, and two unpardonable G's into the finale of the first ballroom scene, just before the final *stretto*, thereby anticipating and destroying the climax Odi il tuon from the sopranos. Madame Tavary still clings to that desolating run up and down the scale with which she contrives to make the conclusion of Non mi dir ridiculous; and Montariol, unable to evade Il mio tesoro by omitting it like Dalla sua pace, did strange things with it in his desperation. His Ottavio was altogether a melancholy performance, as he was put out of countenance from the beginning by being clothed in a seedy misfit which made him look lamentably down on his luck. Mr Harris would not dream of allowing such a costume to be seen on his stage in a modern opera; and I must really urge upon him that there are limits to the application even of the principle that anything is good enough for Mozart.

Maurel's Don Giovanni, though immeasurably better than any we have seen of late years, is not to be compared to his Rigoletto, his Iago, or, in short, to any of his melodramatic parts. Don Juan may be as handsome, as irresistible, as adroit, as unscrupulous, as brave as you please; but the one thing that is not to be tolerated is that he should consciously parade these qualities as if they were elaborate accomplishments instead of his natural parts. And this is exactly where Maurel failed. He gave us a description of Don Juan rather than an impersonation of him. The confident smile, the heroic gesture, the splendid dress, even the intentionally seductive vocal inflexion which made such a success of Là ci darem in spite of Miss de Lussan's coquettish inanity, were all more or less artificial. A Don Juan who is continually aiming at being Don Juan may excite our admiration by the skill with which he does it; but he cannot convince us that he is the real man. I remember seeing Jean de Reszke play the part when he had less than a tenth of Maurel's present skill and experience; and yet I think Mozart would have found the younger man the more sympathetic interpreter.

It seems ungrateful to find fault with an artist who rescues a great role from the hands of such ignoble exponents as the common or Covent Garden Dons who swagger feebly through it like emancipated billiard-markers; but it would hardly be a compliment to Maurel to praise him for so cheap a superiority. And, indeed, there is no fault-finding in the matter. It is a question of temperament. When all is said, the fundamental impossibility remains that Maurel's artistic vein is not Mozartian. One or two points of detail may be mentioned. He was best in the love-making scenes and worst in those with Leporello, whom he treated with a familiarity which was rather that of Robert Macaire with Jacques Strop than of a gentleman with his valet. The scene of the exposure in the ballroom he played rather callously. Nothing in the score is clearer than that Don Juan is discomfited, confused, and at a loss from the moment in which they denounce him until, seeing that there is nothing for it but to fight his way out, he ceases to utter hasty exclamations of dismay, and recovers himself at the words Ma non manca in me coraggio. Maurel dehumanized and melodramatized the scene by missing this entirely, and maintaining a defiant and self-possessed bearing throughout.

And again, on the entry of the statue, which Don Juan, however stable his nerve may be imagined to have been, can hardly have witnessed without at least a dash of surprise and curiosity, Maurel behaved very much as if his uncle had dropped in unexpectedly in the middle of a bachelor's supper-party. The result was that the scene went for nothing, though it is beyond all comparison the most wonderful of the wonders of dramatic music. But if the audience is ever to be cured of the habit of treating it as a sort of voluntary to play them out, it must be very carefully studied by the artist playing Don Juan, upon whose pantomime the whole action of the scene depends, since the statue can only stand with a stony air of weighing several tons, whilst the orchestra makes him as awful as the conductor will allow it. Since Maurel let this scene slip completely through his fingers, I do not see how he can be classed with the great Don Juans (if there ever were any great ones). The problem of how to receive a call from a public statue does not seem to have struck him as worth solving.

The Elvira (Madame Rolla), whose B flat at the end of her aria was perhaps the most excusable of all the inexcusable interpolations, was as good as gold, not indulging once in a scream, and relying altogether on pure vocal tone of remarkable softness. In Mi tradi she succeeded in being more pleasing than any Elvira I can remember except Di Murska, who understood the full value of the part and played it incomparably, like the great artist she was. Madame Rolla does not act with the force of Nilsson; and in the quartet she failed to bring off the effect at the end, where Elvira gets louder and angrier whilst the wretched Don gets more and more agitated by the dread of her making a scene; but I think Maurel was a little unequal to the occasion here too. On the whole, Madame Rolla, whose voice reminds one somewhat of Marimon's, is a useful addition to the company. Mr Harris had better now turn his attention to achieving a really serious performance of Le Nozzi di Figaro.

Richter and Wagner

→>--<←

3 June 1891

THE Richter concerts opened on Monday week with a program the like of which for thrilling novelty has not been heard in London for a long time. The seventh symphony, the Parsifal and Meistersinger preludes, the Ride of the Valkyries: these, with a suite by Bach, were the pledges of the progressive and enterprising spirit that chafes in its protuberant prison-house beneath the great conductor's waistcoat. Seriously – for the finer shades of musical humor are hardly safe with the English public – Richter has no right to stuff a program with the most hackneyed items in his repertory in order to save the trouble of rehearsing. I do not, of course, mean to say that the seventh symphony and the rest should be discarded because they have been performed several times already. But I do mean most emphatically that their execution should be elaborated and perfected every time the public is asked to put its hand in its pocket afresh to hear them. Nothing can be artistically meaner than to trade on the ignorance of those who think that the name of Richter is a guarantee for unimprovable perfection. As a matter of fact, the orchestra is by no means what it ought to be; and it has been getting worse instead of better for some years past.

Let me take an instance or two – always worth a ton of general statement. Every Bayreuth pilgrim is by this time familiar with that wonderful throbbing, fluttering, winnowing cloud of sound which the violins make as the Grail descends in Parsifal. That is to say, the violins ought to make it; but without the most patient and critical preparation they make nothing but a muddle in which the scoffer will justly refuse to recognize anything but a confusion of groups of three notes with groups of four. Now, as prices are high at Richter's concerts, and there is no reason whatever why cheap work should be tolerated there, we are, I consider, entitled to call upon his band either to master this effect or let Parsifal alone. On Monday week they did neither; and the enthusiasm created by the performance of the prelude was due entirely to the extraordinary beauty of that large portion of the work which presents no special difficulties of execution. Why it was immediately followed by the Walkürenritt is more than I can explain. Whether Richter, in a frenzy of contempt for the London musical public, resolved to shew that it had no sense of artistic congruity to be shocked, or whether he took just the opposite view, and thought he would indulge himself with a Mephistophelian joke at its expense, is more than I can guess; but certain it is that the last divine strains of Parsifal were still in our ears when the wild gallop of the Valkyries was upon us with a heathenish riot. And I can unreservedly assure Richter that a more villainous performance of it never was heard before in St James's Hall. To offer us such an orgie of scraping, screeching, banging, and barking as a tone-picture of the daughters of Wotan was an outrage to Wagner. Surely Richter does not conceive Ortlinde, Waltraute, and the rest of them as a parcel of screaming, delirious viragoes, without grace, strength, majesty, or regard for their steeds. For that is the sort of Valkyrie Ride suggested to me by fiddles rasped as if they were whirling grindstones, and trombones overblown until they sound like cracked cornets. Such treatment degrades Wagner to the level of Wiertz, and makes novices guess that Walkürenritt must be German for 'cruelty to animals', which The Meister abhorred with Shelleyan intensity.

I have often enough done justice to Richter's genius as an interpreter both of tone poetry and of absolute music to claim exemption from all suspicion of ill-will towards himself or his school; and I suffer too often from the vapidity of orchestras which, for all their polish, fail miserably whenever sustained tone is needed, to undervalue the example set by the Richter band with its magnificent *sostenuto*. But when it comes to depending on the reputation of the band and the conductor to dispense with careful preparation, and to snatch popular victories with exciting pieces like the Walkürenritt by dint of what I can only describe as instrumental ruffianism, then it is time for every critic whose former praise meant anything but acquiescence in the fashion of admiring Richter, to warn him that unless he promptly takes steps to bring the standard of quality of execution in his orchestra up to that set by the Crystal Palace orchestra, and the standard of exhaustive preparation up to that set by the wonderful performances of Berlioz' works achieved here last winter by the Manchester band, he will lose his old pre-eminence in the estimation of all those who really know the difference between thorough work and scamped work in performing orchestral music of the highest class.

The Wagner birthday concert at Ham House was in many respects a huge improvement on Bayreuth. Twickenham Ferry is an excellent substitute for the Channel or the German Ocean; and the reduction of my travelling expenses from £7 or £8 to 1s. 5½d., and of the time wasted in locomotion from forty hours to one, was highly acceptable. As to comparisons between the country about Richmond and the Fichtelgebirge, or Richmond Park and the Hofgarten, or the view from Richmond Hill and that from the Hohe Warte, it would be ungenerous to Germany to press them. On the other hand, I freely admit that not even the expedient of sending the cornet-player out into the garden before the second part of the concert, to blow the sword motive from The Niblung's Ring, quite made up for the absence of the Wagner Theatre and Parsifal. Lord Dysart did what a man could: he annihilated the very memory of the Theatre Restaurant by a marquee in which I took my sober Wagnerian meal of brown bread and lemonade next to disciples who were trying reckless experiments with *sauerkraut* and rum custard; and he

received us in a house and grounds almost as fit for the purpose
of the afternoon as our own place at Hampton Court. Still, a
house is a house, and a theatre is a theatre, and I strongly urge
Lord Dysart to secede from the useless London branch of the
German Wagner Society, and form a really important English
society with the object of building a Wagner Theatre within
ten minutes' walk of his own door.

The concert was not so good as it might have been had the
singers been able or willing to avail themselves to the fullest
extent of the very favorable conditions for delicate and expressive
vocal art presented by a room in which the weakest singer could
have been heard without the slightest effort. Unfortunately, most
of them seemed rather bent on making a noise; and as the band
was equally anxious to avoid doing so, the result was that the
orchestral part of the concert was better than the vocal part.
Under these circumstances I could not help thinking it rather
cool of Mr Henschel to publicly rebuke a momentary roughness
in the orchestra by making them recommence the prelude to
Wolfram's Blick' ich umher, and then to sing it in the strident
and savagely self-assertive accents of Klingsor, instead of in the
elevated and spiritual style of the poet Wolfram. If I had been
that orchestra, I should have stopped Mr Henschel and made *him*
begin again. Maurel, a southern Frenchman who puts forward
no claim to any special sympathy with Wagner, would never
have inflicted such a misreading on us.

If Mr Henschel had not atoned somewhat by a comparatively
reasonable performance of Wahn, wahn, it would be impossible
to pay him the smallest compliment on his share in the afternoon's proceedings. The only excuse for him is that he is a German – I have long since come to the conclusion that the German
nation labors under a congenial incapacity to understand the
musical side of the universal Wagner. Even Miss Pauline
Cramer, whose sympathy with his sentiment makes her a
genuine enthusiast, and often leads her to find the right musical
expression unconsciously, has failed to see that unless a singer
patiently builds up for herself an eloquent, rich, easy middle to
her voice, and can attack her high notes in all sorts of ways,

quietly or vigorously as the case may demand, half the music of a Wagner part will be lost, and the other half will be apt to produce the general effect of a series of screams. Miss Cramer is so much in earnest, and has such excellent natural gifts – especially a voice which has all the brightness which German voices so commonly lack – that there is no reason why she should not treble her present resources as a lyric and dramatic artist. Her singing of the final scene from the Götterdämmerung was by no means bad; but it was deficient in variety, and cost her more effort than it need have done.

The only orchestral piece performed was the Siegfried Idyll, which has seldom been heard under more suitable conditions (Wagner wrote it, not for public performance, but to serenade his wife with). It went very well, except for a few moments in the middle section, when Mr Armbruster, who has the faults as well as the qualities of an intellect of the most restless and discursive kind, hurried along with mechanical regularity whilst he thought out some remote scientific question, which fortunately did not occupy him very long. On the whole, it was a pleasant half-holiday; and if Lord Dysart would like to give another concert on my birthday, which is due in a month or two, I shall not discourage the project.

Paderewski

>-<

10 June 1891

... AFTER Sarasate's concert came Paderewski's. He gave two concertos – one too many – Beethoven in E flat and Schumann. It was hard on us, and harder on Schumann. I am by no means naturally predisposed to admire Paderewski's style. His master, Leschetitzky, seems to me to have done more to dehumanize pianoforte-playing than any other leading teacher in Europe. When I hear pianists with fingers turned into steel hammers, deliberately murdering Beethoven by putting all sorts of accelerandos and crescendos into his noblest and most steadfast passages, I promptly put them down without further inquiry as pupils of Leschetitzky.

Paderewski's excessive hardness of touch, which tells even when he is playing with the most exquisite lightness, and which must be referred to his master rather than to himself, would limit him seriously if his exceptional comprehensiveness as a musician did not enable him to seize about ten points of treatment in a composition for every one that comes within the range of the ordinary pianist. He plays the Schumann concerto, for instance, so intelligently that if I were told that he was the composer, and did not know to the contrary, I could easily believe it, although I should be surprised at any composer having submitted to such an arduous technical training as he has evidently undergone. In spite of Leschetitzky, then, the concert, though a tiring one from its inordinate length, was real and interesting throughout.

Paderewski treated the orchestra better than they treated him; for he played with an unfailing sense of the relation of the solo part to the rest, whereas they, in their one great opportunity – the first allegro of the Beethoven concerto – played roughly and hastily, a misfortune for which the chief blame must lie upon Mr Henschel who handled this beautiful movement with a want of tenderness which was at times almost brutal. It is a pity that so able and modern-spirited a musician as he should repeatedly provoke remonstrances of this sort from critics who would much rather help than hinder his influence as a conductor and musical *entrepreneur*. As to Paderewski himself, I have only one demurrer to put in. I maintain that the great octave passage which occupies twenty bars or so of the middle section of that first movement, should be given in an unwavering fortissimo until the point when it breaks up and melts like a cloud. Paderewski made a marked crescendo in all the ascending passages, and thereby reduced the whole trait to a mere commonplace. Save for this Leschetitzkyism, I unreservedly congratulate him on his concert. . . .

Messiah

>+>+<+

1 July 1891

FUNDAMENTALLY my view of the Handel Festival is that of a convinced and ardent admirer of Handel. My favorite oratorio is The Messiah, with which I have spent many of the hours which others give to Shakespear, or Scott, or Dickens. But for all this primary bias in favor of Handel, my business is still to be that of the critic, who, invited to pronounce an opinion on the merits of a performance by four thousand executants, must judge these abnormal conditions by their effect on the work as open-mindedly as if there were only four hundred, or forty, or four. And I am bound to add that he who, so judging, delivers a single and unqualified verdict on the Festival, stultifies himself. The very same conditions which make one choral number majestic, imposing, even sublime, make another heavy, mechanical, meaningless. For instance, no host could be too mighty for the Hallelujah Chorus, or See the Conquering Hero. In them every individual chorister knows without study or instruction what he has to do and how he has to feel. The impulse to sing spreads even to the audience; and those who are old hands at choral singing do not always restrain it.

I saw more than one of my neighbors joining in the Hallelujah on the first day; and if my feelings at that moment had permitted me to make a properly controlled artistic effort, I think I should have been no more able to remain silent than Santley was. Under the circumstances, however, I followed the example of Albani, who, knowing that she had to save her voice for I know that my Redeemer liveth, kept a vocal score tightly on her mouth the whole time, and looked over it with the expression of a child confronted with some intolerably tempting sweetmeat which it knows it must not touch.

But The Messiah is not all Hallelujah. Compare such a moment as I have just described with the experience of listening

to the fiercely tumultuous He trusted in God, with its alterna-
tions of sullen mockery with high-pitched derision, and its
savage shouts of Let him deliver him if he delight in him, jog-
ging along at about half the proper speed, with an expression of
the deepest respect and propriety, as if a large body of the leading
citizens, headed by the mayor, were presenting a surpassingly
dull address to somebody. There may be, in the way of the
proper presentation of such a chorus as this, something of the
difficulty which confronted Wagner at the rehearsals of Tannhäuser in Paris in 1861, when he asked the ballet master to make
his forces attack the Bacchanal in a bacchanalian way. 'I understand perfectly what you mean,' said the functionary; 'but only
to a whole ballet of *premiers sujets* dare I breathe such sug-
gestions.'

No doubt Mr Manns's three thousand five hundred choristers
might better his instructions so heartily as to go considerably
beyond the utmost licence of art if he told them that unless they
sang that chorus like a howling bloodthirsty mob, the utter
loneliness of Thy rebuke hath broken his heart, and Behold and
see, must be lost, and with it the whole force of the tragic climax
of the oratorio. Besides which, there is the physical difficulty,
which only a skilled and powerful orator could fully surmount,
of giving instruction of that kind to such a host. But I see no
reason why matters should not be vastly improved if Mr Manns
would adopt throughout the bolder policy as to speed which was
forced on him after four on Selection day by the silent urgency
of the clock, and persisted in to some extent – always with convincing effect – in Israel. Increased speed, however, is not all
that is wanted. To get rid completely of the insufferable lumber-
ing which is the curse of English Handelian choral singing, a
spirited reform in style is needed.

For instance, Handel, in his vigorous moods, is fond of
launching the whole mass of voices into florid passages of great
brilliancy and impetuosity. In one of the most splendid choruses
in The Messiah, For He shall purify the sons of Levi, the
syllable 'fy' comes out in a single trait consisting of no less than
thirty-two semiquavers. That trait should be sung with one im-

pulse from end to end without an instant's hesitation. How is it actually done in England? Just as if the thirty-two semiquavers were eight bars of crochets taken *alla breve* in a not very lively tempo. The effect, of course, is to make the chorus so dull that all the reputation of Handel is needed to persuade Englishmen that they ought to enjoy it, whilst Frenchmen go away from our festivals confirmed in their scepticism as to our pet musical classic. When I had been listening for some minutes on Wednesday to the festival choristers trudging with ludicrous gravity through what they called Tellit Outa Mongthe Hea-ea Then, I could not help wishing that Santley, who roused them to boundless enthusiasm by his singing of Why do the nations, had given them a taste of their own quality by delivering those chains of triplets on the words 'rage' and 'counsel', as quavers in twelve-eight time in the tempo of the pastoral symphony. The celestial Lift up your heads, O ye gates, lost half its triumphant exultation from this heaviness of gait.

Again, in the beginning of For unto us, the tenors and basses told each other the news in a prosaic, methodical way which made the chorus quite comic until the thundering Wonderful, Counsellor, one of Handel's mightiest strokes, was reached; and even here the effect was disappointing, because the chorus, having held nothing in reserve, could make no climax. The orchestra needed at that point about twenty more of the biggest of big drums. Another lost opportunity was the pathetically grand conclusion of All we like sheep. Nothing in the whole work needs to be sung with more intense expression than But the Lord hath laid on Him the iniquity of us all. Unless it sounds as if the singers were touched to their very hearts, they had better not sing it at all. On that Monday it came as mechanically as if the four entries of the voices had been produced by drawing four stops in an organ. This was the greater pity, because it must be conceded to our young Handel-sceptics that the preceding musical portraiture of the sheep going astray has no great claims on their reverence.

I am aware that many people who feel the shortcomings of our choral style bear with it under the impression, first, that the English people are naturally too slow and shy in their musical ways, and, second, that *bravura* vocalization and impetuous speed are not possible or safe with large choruses. To this I reply, first, that the natural fault of the English when they are singing with genuine feeling is not slowness, but rowdiness, as the neighbors of the Salvation Army know; second, that it would undoubtedly be as risky to venture far in the *bravura* direction with a very small chorus as to attempt the Walküre fire-music or Liszt's Mazeppa in an ordinary theatre orchestra with its little handful of strings. But both these compositions are safe with sixteen first and sixteen second violins, because, though notes are dropped and mistakes made, they are not all made simultaneously, and the result is that at any given instant an overwhelming majority of the violins are right. For the same reason, I do not see why nine hundred basses, even if they were the stiffest and slowest in the world, could not be safely sent at full speed in the *bravura* style through Handel's easy diatonic semiquaver traits, as safely as our violinists are now sent through Wagner's demisemi-quavers.

So much for the compatibility of speed with accuracy. As to safety, I need only appeal to the results achieved by Mr Manns on Friday, when he got away from The Messiah, which is too sentimental for him, to Israel, which is far more congenial to his temperament. The only choral number in this which was quite unsatisfactory was I will exalt Him, and here the shortcoming was made unavoidable by the peculiar style of the chorus, since it – like And with His stripes in the Messiah – requires a beauty of execution which would suffice for a mass by Palestrina, and which is out of the question under Handel Festival conditions. The other choruses were spirited and forcible – some of them magnificent. He gave them hailstones, But the waters overwhelmed, and The horse and his rider were tremendous: one felt after them that the festival had justified its existence beyond all cavil.

If these criticisms are to bear any fruit in raising the festival performances of The Messiah to a typical artistic perfection – a result which I believe to be quite possible, and certainly well worth striving for – they must be weighed, not by Mr Manns or the Crystal Palace authorities, but by the local conductors throughout the country, who coach their contingents in the work, and send them up with preconceived ideas as to its execution which Mr Manns is powerless to change or even greatly to modify. Every contingent trained by a mere organist, to whom The Messiah is but a part of the drudgery of his professional routine, is simply a nuisance on the Handel orchestra. And every contingent trained by an artist who ranks the work among his treasures, and part of whose artistic ambition it is to hear at last in England a really adequate performance of it, is, as Judas Maccabaeus says, 'a thousand men'.

Otello

→-◄◄

22 July 1891

I CONFESS to having witnessed with a certain satisfaction the curious demonstrations which enlivened the first performance of Otello at Covent Garden. The first sign of tumult was a disposition to insist on applauding Maurel in season and out of season, even to the extent of causing ridiculous interruptions to the performance. The second was an almost equally strong disposition to disparage – I had almost said to hoot – Jean de Reszke, who was defended by vehement counter-demonstrations, in leading which Lassalle, standing in a box next the stage on the grand tier, was the most conspicuous figure. Fortunately, the majority in an English audience generally declines to concern itself in green-room politics; and at Covent Garden the majority is so huge that it is not possible to make much of a scene there. By the end of the second act matters relapsed into the usual routine, greatly, I should imagine, to the relief of Maurel. However, partial as the demonstration was, it was far too general to be the work of a claque; and I recommend it to the most serious consideration of Brother Jean. It is to his petulant laziness, and to nothing else, that we owe the frightful waste of artistic resources at Covent Garden on stale repetitions of worn-out operas night after night, when we might have been listening to Siegfried and Otello, not to mention half a dozen other works which are familiar in every second-rate German town, and of which we know nothing in London. The height of his ambition would be attained, as far as one can judge, if he were permitted to maintain his status as leading tenor at the Royal Italian Opera by a single performance of Romeo every year, leaving the rest of the work to be done by Perotti, Montariol, and Ravelli. And yet, at the beginning of this season, he had the – shall I say the ingenuousness? – to favor an interviewer with some observations about his devotion to Art. Can he wonder at the frequenters of the Opera shewing a little temper in the matter at last?

His acting as Otello was about equally remarkable for its amateurish ineptitudes and for its manifestations of the natural histrionic powers which he has so studiously neglected for the last fifteen years. Though he overcame his genius for being late so far as to get on the stage punctually for his first utterance in the storm, it reconquered him when he entered to interrupt the fight between Cassio and Montano; and in his sudden appearance at the masked door in Desdemona's bedroom, which depended for its effect on being timed exactly to a certain chord, he was a good half bar behindhand. His reluctance to determined physical action came out chiefly in his onslaught on Iago, which he managed in such a way as to make the audience feel how extremely obliging it was of Maurel to fall. And at the end of the third act, in simulating the epileptic fit in which Otello's fury culminates, he moved the gods to laughter by lying down with a much too obvious solicitude for his own comfort.

On the whole it may be said that throughout the first two acts his diffidence and irresolution again and again got the better of his more vigorous and passionate impulses. This was intensified no doubt by nervousness; but it was partly due also to his halting between a half-hearted attempt at the savage style of Tamagno and the quieter, more refined manner natural to himself. In the third act, when the atmosphere of the house had become friendly, he began to treat the part more in his own fashion, and at last got really into it, playing for the first time with sustained conviction instead of merely with fitful bursts of self-assertion. Indeed, but for that gingerly fall at the end, this third act would have been an unqualified success for him. As it was, it shewed, like his Don Jose and other post-Van Dyck performances, that when the rivalry of younger men and the decay of his old superficial charm with advancing years force him to make the most of all his powers, he may yet gain more as an actor than he will lose as a singer.

His Otello will never be like Tamagno's; but he need not regret that, as the same thing might have been said of Salvini. The Italian tenor's shrill screaming voice and fierce temper were tremendously effective here and there; but the nobler side of the Moor, which Salvini brought out with such admirable artistic quietude and self-containment, and which De Reszke shews a considerable, though only half cultivated, power of indicating in the same way, was left untouched by Tamagno, who on this and other accounts is the very last man a wise tenor would attempt to imitate.

There is less to be said as to the other principals. It is no compliment to Albani to declare that she was better than Madame Cattaneo, as she could hardly have been worse. Like De Reszke, she redeemed herself in the latter half of the opera. Her intonation improved; and her acting had the sincerity which so honorably distinguishes her from most of her rivals, and which so often leads her straight to the right vocal treatment of purely dramatic music. If she will only forgo that absurd little stage run with which she embraces Otello in the first act, she will have nothing to reproach herself with as far as her playing of the part is concerned. Maurel, tired out as to voice, dropping all the G's; and unable to make the pianissimo nuances tell at anything softer than a tolerably vigorous *mezzo forte*, was yet able to repeat his old success as Iago. His playing is as striking and picturesque as ever; but I have come to think that it requires a touch of realism here and there to relieve its somewhat mechanical grace and effectiveness. The excessive descriptiveness which is the fault in his method, and even in his conception of the actor's function, resulting in a tendency to be illustrative rather than impersonative, occasionally leads him to forget the natural consequences of the actions he represents on the stage.

For instance, when Otello half throttles Iago, it is a little disillusioning to see the victim rise from a faultless attitude, and declaim Divina grazia, difendimi, with his throat in perfect order. Nothing is easier to produce than the *voce soffocata*; and there are not many operatic passages in which it is more appropriate than here. Apart from these matters of detail, the chief objection to Maurel's Iago is that it is not Iago at all, but rather the Caesar Borgia of romance. As far as it is human, it is a portrait of a distinguished officer, one who would not be passed over for Cassio when he was expecting his step. I am aware that this view of him falls in with the current impression in artistic circles that Iago was a very fine fellow. But in circles wherein men have to take one another seriously, there will not be much difference of opinion as to the fact that Iago must have been an ingrained blackguard and consequently an (if I may use a slightly Germanic adjective) obviously-to-everyone-but-himself-unpromotable person.

A certain bluffness and frankness, with that habit of looking you straight in the face which is the surest sign of a born liar, male or female, appear to me to be indispensable to 'honest Iago'; and it is the absence of these, with the statuesque attitudes, the lofty carriage of the head, and the delicate play of the hands and wrists, that makes the figure created by Maurel irreconcilable with my notion of the essentially vulgar ancient who sang comic songs to Cassio and drank him, so to speak, under the table. There is too much of Lucifer, the fallen angel, about it – and this, be it remarked, by no means through the fault of Verdi, who has in several places given a quite Shakespearean tone to the part by *nuances* which Maurel refuses to execute, a striking instance being the famous Ecco il leon at the end of the fourth act, when Iago spurns the insensible body of the prostrate Otello.

Nobody, it seems to me, can escape the meaning of the descent to the rattling shake on the middle F which Verdi has written. It expresses to perfection the base envious exultation of the ass's kick at the helpless lion, and suggests nothing of the Satanic scorn with which Maurel, omitting the ugly shake, leaves the stage. His performance is to be admired rather as a powerfully executed fantasy of his own than as the Iago either of Verdi or Shakespear. If his successors in the part try to imitate him, their wisdom will be even less than their originality.

It remains to get through the most melancholy part of my task – the criticism of the staging of the opera : I need hardly say that what money could secure in the way of scenery and dresses has been secured, and that amply. But money alone does not go very far in the first act of Otello, which stands or falls by the naturalness of the delightful scene where the storm subsides, the thunder dies out of the air, and there begins that merry scene round the bonfire which is perhaps Verdi's freshest and prettiest piece of descriptive music. Its total failure at Covent Garden was a foregone conclusion. I should be sorry to assail any such hard-worked body as the Covent Garden chorus with so un-graceful an epithet as pigheaded; but really if they could have seen themselves standing just clear of the pale flame of that miserable penn'orth of methylated spirit, staring at Mancinelli, and bawling without a ray of feeling for what they were sup-posed to be doing, they would not venture to defend themselves against any extremity of abuse. The scene was so effectually extinguished in consequence, that those who had seen the Scala people at the Lyceum were to be heard in all directions during the interval naïvely declaring that they found the first act very dull now that the novelty of the work had worn off. The final outrage of the stage-manager (if there is really any such func-tionary at Covent Garden) was the turning on in the sky of a most outrageous constellation, intended, I think, for the Great Bear, and consisting of gas lamps of the first magnitude and of aggressive yellowness. I remember believing implicitly in the reality of everything I saw on the stage at my first pantomime; but even then I do not think I should have been taken in by such incredible heavenly bodies as these. They achieved a sort of *succès de rire* by winking at the most rapturous part of the duet which De Reszke and Albani were carrying on below in happy ignorance of the facetiousness of the firmament; but, though I could not help laughing, I strongly recommend Mr Harris to send down to Greenwich for an expert to superintend this part of the opera before he repeats it.

It cannot be said, unfortunately, that the tediousness stopped after the first act, although the stage-manager's opportunities ceased then. The tact, steadiness, and – when needed – the authority with which Faccio brought Otello through at the Lyceum without letting it flag for a second was beyond the powers of the amiable and enthusiastic Mancinelli. He shewed his usual feeling for the orchestral points; but, on the other hand, he let things drag terribly, particularly in the third act, by waiting for singers who were waiting for him, and often choosing unnecessarily slow *tempi* to start with. In the second act he astonished Maurel by taking the applause at the end of the Credo as an encore – an unheard-of artistic mistake; and, shortly afterwards, he astonished De Reszke still more by doing exactly the reverse after the Ora per sempre addio, sante memorie. On the whole, if he could have borrowed a little of Bevignani's disposition to whack an opera along, without also acquiring his characteristic imperviousness, Otello would have been over sooner, and the audience would have gone home with a better opinion of the work.

The Mozart Centenary

→-◄◄

9 December 1891

THE Mozart Centenary has made a good deal of literary and musical business this week. Part of this is easy enough, especially for the illustrated papers. Likenesses of Mozart at all ages; view of Salzburg; portrait of Marie Antoinette (described in the text as 'the ill-fated'), to whom he proposed marriage at an early age; picture of the young composer, two and a half feet high, crushing the Pompadour with his 'Who is this woman that refuses to kiss me? The Queen kissed me! (Sensation)'; facsimile of the original MS. of the first four bars of Là ci darem, and the like. These, with copious paraphrases of the English translation of Otto Jahn's great biography, will pull the journalists proper through the Centenary with credit. The critic's task is not quite so easy.

The word is, of course, Admire, admire, admire; but unless you frankly trade on the ignorance of the public, and cite as illustrations of his unique genius feats that come easily to dozens of organists and choir-boys who never wrote, and never will write, a bar of original music in their lives; or pay his symphonies and operas empty compliments that might be transferred word for word, without the least incongruity, to the symphonies of Spohr and the operas of Offenbach; or represent him as composing as spontaneously as a bird sings, on the strength of his habit of perfecting his greater compositions in his mind before he wrote them down – unless you try these well-worn dodges, you will find nothing to admire that is peculiar to Mozart: the fact being that he, like Praxiteles, Raphael, Molière or Shakespear, was no leader of a new departure or founder of a school.

He came at the end of a development, not at the beginning of one; and although there are operas and symphonies, and even pianoforte sonatas and pages of instrumental scoring of his, on which you can put your finger and say, 'Here is final perfection in this manner; and nobody, whatever his genius may be, will ever get a step further on these lines,' you cannot say, 'Here is an entirely new vein of musical art, of which nobody ever dreamt before Mozart.' Haydn, who made the mould for Mozart's symphonies, was proud of Mozart's genius because he felt his own part in it: he would have written the E flat symphony if he could, and, though he could not, was at least able to feel that the man who had reached that pre-eminence was standing on his old shoulders. Now, Haydn would have recoiled from the idea of composing – or perpetrating, as he would have put it – the first movement of Beethoven's Eroica, and would have repudiated all part in leading music to such a pass.

The more far-sighted Gluck not only carried Mozart in his arms to within sight of the goal of his career as an opera composer, but even cleared a little of the new path into which Mozart's finality drove all those successors of his who were too gifted to waste their lives in making weak dilutions of Mozart's scores and serving them up as 'classics'. Many Mozart worshippers cannot bear to be told that their hero was not the founder of a dynasty. But in art the highest success is to be the last of your race, not the first. Anybody, almost, can make a beginning: the difficulty is to make an end – to do what cannot be bettered.

For instance, if the beginner were to be ranked above the consummator, we should, in literary fiction, have to place Captain Mayne Reid, who certainly struck a new vein, above Dickens, who simply took the novel as he found it, and achieved the feat of compelling his successor (whoever he may be), either to create quite another sort of novel, or else to fall behind his predecessor as at best a superfluous imitator. Surely, if so great a composer as Haydn could say, out of his greatness as a man, 'I am not the best of my school, though I was the first,' Mozart's worshippers can afford to acknowledge, with equal gladness of spirit, that their hero was not the first, though he was the best. It is always like that. Praxiteles, Raphael, and Co., have great men for their pioneers, and only fools for their followers.

So far everybody will agree with me. This proves either that I am hopelessly wrong or that the world has had at least half a century to think the matter over in. And, sure enough, a hundred years ago, Mozart was considered a desperate innovator: it was his reputation in this respect that set so many composers – Meyerbeer, for example – cultivating innovation for its own sake. Let us, therefore, jump a hundred years forward, right up to date, and see whether there is any phenomenon of the same nature in view today. We have not to look far. Here, under our very noses, is Wagner held up on all hands as the founder of a school and the arch-musical innovator of our age. He himself knew better; but since his death I appear to be the only person who shares his view of the matter. I assert with the utmost confidence that in 1991 it will be seen quite clearly that Wagner was the end of the nineteenth-century, or Beethoven school, instead of the beginning of the twentieth-century school; just as Mozart's most perfect music is the last word of the eighteenth century, and not the first of the nineteenth. It is none the less plain because everyone knows that Il Seraglio was the beginning of the school of nineteenth-century German operas of Mozart, Beethoven, Weber, and Wagner; that Das Veilchen is the beginning of the nineteenth-century German song of Schubert, Mendelssohn, and Schumann; and that Die Zauberflöte is the ancestor, not only of the Ninth Symphony, but of the Wagnerian allegorical music-drama, with personified abstractions instead of individualized characters as *dramatis personae*. But Il Seraglio and Die Zauberflöte do not belong to the group of works which constitute Mozart's consummate achievement – Don Juan, Le Nozze di Figaro, and his three or four perfect symphonies. They are nineteenth-century music heard advancing in the distance, as his Masses are seventeenth-century music retreating in the distance. And, similarly, though the future fossiliferous critics of 1991, after having done their utmost, without success, to crush twentieth-century music, will be able to shew that Wagner (their chief classic) made one or two experiments in that direction, yet the world will rightly persist in thinking of him as a characteristically nineteenth-century composer of the school of Beethoven, greater than Beethoven by as much as Mozart was greater than Haydn. And now I hope I have saved my reputation by saying something at which everybody will exclaim, 'Bless me! what nonsense!' Nevertheless, it is true; and our would-be Wagners had better look to it; for all their efforts to exploit the apparently inexhaustible wealth of musical material opened up at Bayreuth only prove that Wagner used it up to the last ounce, and that secondhand Wagner is more insufferable, because usually more pretentious, than even secondhand Mozart used to be.

For my own part, if I do not care to rhapsodize much about Mozart, it is because I am so violently prepossessed in his favor that I am capable of supplying any possible deficiency in his work by my imagination. Gounod has devoutly declared that Don Giovanni has been to him all his life a revelation of perfection, a miracle, a work without fault. I smile indulgently at

Gounod, since I cannot afford to give myself away so generously (there being, no doubt, less of me); but I am afraid my fundamental attitude towards Mozart is the same as his. In my small-boyhood I by good luck had an opportunity of learning the Don thoroughly, and if it were only for the sense of the value of fine workmanship which I gained from it, I should still esteem that lesson the most important part of my education. Indeed, it educated me artistically in all sorts of ways, and disqualified me only in one – that of criticizing Mozart fairly. Everyone appears a sentimental, hysterical bungler in comparison when anything brings his finest work vividly back to me. Let me take warning by the follies of Oublicheff, and hold my tongue. . . .

Incidental Music

⤖⤙

27 January 1892

I HAVE seldom been more astonished than I was last week, when the manager of the Haymarket Theatre offered me an opportunity of hearing the music which Mr Henschel has just composed for Hamlet. Not only had I never heard of a tragedian regarding incidental music as having any interest separable in the remotest degree from his own performance, or as being a less mechanical part of that than the last touch of paint or limelight, but I had been brought up to believe that Hamlet in its natural state consisted musically of the march from Judas Maccabaeus for the entry of the Court, and the Dead March in Saul for Hamlet's death, the *entr'actes* being selected from no longer popular overtures such as La Sirène, etc. My opinion of Mr Tree consequently rose to such a pitch as to all but defeat the object of my visit to the last rehearsal; for instead of listening to Mr Henschel's interludes, I spent the intervals in explaining to Mr Tree exactly how his part ought to be played, he listening with the patience and attention which might be expected from so accomplished an actor. However, I heard enough with one ear to serve my purpose.

What Mr Henschel has done with his opportunity cannot be described off-hand to those who have never thought over the position of the composer in the theatre. For him there are two extremes. One is to assume the full dignity of the creative musician, and compose an independent overture which, however sympathetic it may be with the impending drama, nevertheless takes the forms proper to pure music, and is balanced and finished as a beautiful and symmetrical fabric of sounds, performable as plain Opus 1000 apart from the drama, as satisfactorily as the drama is performed apart from it. Example: Egmont, in which Beethoven and Goethe associate as peers in their diverse arts, Beethoven not merely illustrating Goethe's masterpiece but adding a masterpiece of his own on the same subject. The other extreme is to supply bare *mélodrame*, familiar samples of which may be found in the ethereal strains from muted violins which accompany the unfolding of transformation scenes in pantomimes, the animated measures which enliven the rallies in the harlequinade, or the weird throbbings of the ghost melody in The Corsican Brothers.

The production of these is not musical composition: it is mere musical tailoring, in the course of which the *mélodrame* is cut and made to the measure of the stage business, and altered by snipping or patching when it comes to be tried on at rehearsal. The old-fashioned actor got his practical musical education in this way; and he will tell you that certain speeches are easy to speak 'through music' and frightfully hard without it; or, as Richard III, he will work himself up to the requisite pitch of truculence in the 'Who intercepts me in my expedition?' scene, partly by listening to the trumpets, and partly by swearing at them for not playing louder.

Beyond this he is so untutored that he will unhesitatingly call upon the *chef d'orchestra* to 'stop that music' in the very middle of a suspension, or with a promising first inversion of the common chord, or on a dominant seventh or the like, quite unconscious of the risk of some musician rising in the theatre on the first night and saying, 'I beg your pardon for interrupting you, sir; but will you kindly ask the band to resolve that four-to-three before you proceed with your soliloquy?' The idea that music is written in sentences with full stops at the end of them, just as much as dramatic poetry is, does not occur to him: all he knows is that he cannot make the audience shudder or feel sentimental without music, exactly as the comedian knows that he cannot make the audience laugh unless the lights are full on. And the music man at the theatre seldom counts for more than a useful colleague of the gas man.

This state of things at last gives way to evolutionary forces like other states of things. The rage for culture opens a career for cultivated men (not merely cultivated players) as theatrical managers and actors; and the old-fashioned actors and managers find themselves compelled by stress of competition to pose as connoisseurs in all the arts, and to set up Medicean retinues of literary advisers, poets, composers, artists, archaeologists, and even critics. And whenever a masterpiece of dramatic literature is revived, the whole retinue is paraded. Now the very publicity of the parade makes it impossible for the retinue to be too servile: indeed, to the full extent to which it reflects lustre on the manager can it also insist on having a voice in the artistic conduct of his enterprises.

Take the composer, for instance. No actor-manager could tell Sir Arthur Sullivan to 'stop that music', or refuse to allow Mr Henschel to resolve his dischords. On the other hand, no manager will engage an orchestra of from eighty to a hundred performers for an overture and *entr'actes*; and no actor will sacrifice any of the effectiveness of his business in order to fit it to the music; whilst at the same time the actor-manager expects all the most modern improvements in the way of 'leading motives', which make excellent material for press-cuttings. The situation being thus limited, the composer submits to become a musical tailor as far as the *mélodrame* is concerned, but throws over the manager completely in the overture and *entr'actes* by composing them with a view to performance as 'an orchestral suite' at the Crystal Palace or London Symphony concerts, laying himself out frankly for a numerous orchestra and a silent audience, instead of for a theatre band contending feebly with the chatter of the dramatic critics. Clearly he might venture upon a great overture like Egmont or Coriolan but for the modern improvements – the leading motives – which are an implied part of his contract. The tragedian must have his motive; and the leading lady, even when she is not the most influential person in the theatre, is allowed to have one also as a foil to the tragedian's. Macduff, Richmond, and Laertes will soon advance their claims, which are obviously no more valid than those of high-reaching Buckingham, Duncan, Polonius, and Claudius.

Mark my words: as actors come to understand these things better, we shall have such scenes at rehearsal as have never before been witnessed in a theatre – Rosencrantz threatening to throw up his part because his motive is half a bar shorter than Guildenstern's; the Ghost claiming, on Mozart's authority, an absolute monopoly of the trombones; Hamlet asking the composer, with magnificent politeness, whether he would mind doubling the basses with a *contrafagotto* in order to bring out the Inky Cloak theme a little better; Othello insisting on being in the bass and Olivia on being in the treble when their themes are worked simultaneously with those of Iago and Viola, and the wretched composer finally writing them all in double counterpoint in order that each may come uppermost or undermost by turns....

Miss Osmond

24 February 1892

MISS OSMOND, who appeared at Steinway Hall on the 16th, is a young English pianist who has studied in England from first to last, which is at present, I am sorry to say, a course rather patriotic than wise. Miss Osmond has exceptional agility of finger; and this has led her, apparently, to depend for success chiefly on her ability to strike all the notes in florid compositions of the Balakireff type with great rapidity. But I recommend Miss Osmond to go abroad for awhile, after all. Not that she will find better teachers there; but she will find places where a young lady can, without excessive expense or scandal, spend enough of her life in the opera-house and the concert-room to educate herself musically – an end not to be gained by any quantity of pianism alone. For her fault now is that her pianism has outstripped her musicianship; and it is but too likely that this is due to her misfortune in living in a country where you cannot have even a cheap piano provided for the children to march to in a Board School without some mean millionaire or other crying out that the rates will ruin him. . . .

Joachim and Schubert

→>-<←

23 March 1892

SOME alarm was created at the Crystal Palace on the 12th by the announcement that 'Professor Joseph Joachim' was to play Max Bruch's latest violin concerto. At a time when all the best friends of art are striving to turn our professors into artists, it seemed too bad to turn one of our greatest artists into a professor. However, he did not play in the least like one. His artistic conscience is as sensitive and as untiring as ever; his skill is not diminished; and his physical endurance proved equal to a severe test in a quick movement – practically a *moto perpetuo* – by Bach. Bruch's concerto, like most of his works, is masterly in the most artificial vulgarities of the grandiose, the passionate, the obviously sentimental, and the coarsely impulsive. Those partisans of Joachim who contend for his superiority to all other violinists (that is the worst of your amateur critic: he or she always has a Dulcinea whose charms are to be maintained against all comers) are fond of proclaiming the severity of his taste. He knows, they tell us, all the fantasias and the claptrap to which Sarasate and Isaÿe condescend, and can execute them superbly; but he refuses to play any music in public that is not of the very highest class. Then, I ask, why does he play Max Bruch?

I do not, of course, address the question to Joachim himself, since I know better than to hold any artist responsible for everything that his devotees ascribe to him; but I do ask it of the devotees themselves, with a view to instructing them a little as to qualitative as distinct from formal differences in music. It is true that Joachim does not go down to the Crystal Palace with a set of variations by Ernst, and entertain the audience by mimicking the whistling of the piccolo with his harmonics. But if Ernst's variations were as good as those in a Bach chaconne, Joachim would put them at the head of his repertory. The difference is not in the variation form, but in the quality of the music.

Now, if you overlook the difference in form between Bruch's concertos and the fantasias which Sarasate plays so admirably, and compare the quality of the music only, you will end by exclaiming that a violinist who plays Bruch may play anything – variations on the Carnival of Venice, Home Sweet Home on one string, or what you please. Let us make up our minds comfortably that the writing of a piece in three movements in sonata form does not add a cubit to its stature. Otherwise we shall have every composer who finds himself inspired with barely matter enough for a fantasia, spinning it out into a concerto in order that it may lie upon the same shelf with the work of Beethoven and Mendelssohn, and so come under Joachim's notice. In dramatic literature it is now generally understood that an author is not to rush into five acts and blank verse if he can possibly help it; and the result is that nobody now confuses the born vaudeville writers with the great dramatic poets.

But in music there is still a general impression that the form makes the composer, and not the composer the form. Bruch's Scottish fantasia is much better than his concertos; but it is on the strength of the concertos that he is regarded as a sort of contemporary old master, and played by the severe Joachim. By the way, if we must always have concertos, could we not have a little more variety in them? I seem to be for ever listening to Mendelssohn, Beethoven, Bruch, and Brahms; whilst Mozart, Spohr, and Wieniawski are numbered with the dead.

At the Crystal Palace there is an understanding among the regular frequenters that a performance of Schubert's Symphony in C is one of the specialities of the place. The analytic program of it is one of Sir George Grove's masterpieces; and Mr Manns always receives a special ovation at the end. The band rises to the occasion with its greatest splendor; and I have to make a point of looking interested and pleased, lest Sir George should turn my way, and, reading my inmost thoughts, cut me dead for ever afterwards. For it seems to me all but wicked to give the public so irresistible a description of all the manifold charms and winningnesses of this astonishing symphony, and not tell them, on the other side of the question, the lamentable truth that a more exasperatingly brainless composition was never put on paper. Fresh as I was this time from the Rossini centenary, I could not help thinking, as I listened to those outrageously overdone and often abortive climaxes in the last movement, how much better than Schubert the wily composer of Tancredi could engineer this sort of sensationalism. It was not only his simple mechanism and the infallible certainty with which it wound you up to striking-point in exactly sixteen bars: it was his cool appreciation of the precise worth of the trick when he had done it.

Poor Schubert, who laughed at Rossini's overtures, and even burlesqued them, here lays out crescendo after crescendo, double after quickstep, gallopade after gallopade, with an absurdly sincere and excited conviction that if he only hurries fast enough he will presently overtake Mozart and Beethoven, who are not to be caught up in a thousand miles by any man with second-rate brains, however wonderful his classical endowment. Much as I appreciate the doughtiness with which Sir George Grove fought Schubert's battle in England, yet now that it is won I instinctively bear back a little, feeling that before any artist, whatever his branch may be, can take his place with the highest, there is a certain price to be paid in head-work, and that Schubert never paid that price. Let that be admitted, and we may play the Symphony in C until we are all black in the face: I shall not be the first to tire of it. . . .

Brahms's Clarinet Quintet

11 May 1892

ONLY the other day I remarked that I was sure to come across Brahms' new clarionet quintet sooner or later. And, sure enough, my fate overtook me last week at Mr G. Clinton's Wind Concert at Steinway Hall. I shall not attempt to describe this latest exploit of the Leviathan Maunderer. It surpassed my utmost expectations: I never heard such a work in my life. Brahms' enormous gift of music is paralleled by nothing on earth but Mr Gladstone's gift of words: it is a verbosity which outfaces its own commonplaceness by dint of sheer magnitude. The first movement of the quintet is the best; and had the string players been on sufficiently easy terms with it, they might have softened it and given effect to its occasional sentimental excursions into dreamland. Unluckily they were all preoccupied with the difficulty of keeping together; and they were led by a violinist whose bold, free, slashing style, though useful in a general way, does more harm than good when the strings need to be touched with great tenderness and sensitiveness.

Mr Clinton played the clarinet part with scrupulous care, but without giving any clue to his private view of the work, which, though it shews off the compass and contrasts the registers of the instrument in the usual way, contains none of the haunting phrases which Weber, for instance, was able to find for the expression of its idiosyncrasy. The presto of the third movement is a ridiculously dismal version of a lately popular hornpipe. I first heard it at the pantomime which was produced at Her Majesty's Theatre a few years ago; and I have always supposed it to be a composition of Mr Solomon's. Anyhow, the street-pianos went through an epidemic of it; and it certainly deserved a merrier fate than burying alive in a Brahms quintet. . . .

Siegfried under Mahler

›‑‹

15 June 1892

LAST Wednesday I was told that Siegfried was to be produced that evening at Covent Garden. I was incredulous, and asked my informant whether he did not mean Carmen, with Miss Zélie de Lussan in the title part. He said he thought not. I suggested Faust, Les Huguenots, even Die Meistersinger; but he stuck to his story: Siegfried, he said, was really and truly in the bills, and the house was sold out. Still doubting, I went to the box-office, where they confirmed the intelligence, except that they had just one stall left. I took it, and went away wondering and only half convinced. But when I reached the theatre in the evening a little late, fully expecting to find notices on the seats to the effect that Siegfried was unavoidably postponed, in consequence of the sudden indisposition of the dragon, the Philémon and Cavalleria substituted, I found the lights out and the belated stall-holders wandering like ghosts through the gloom in search of their numbers, helped only by the glimmer from the huge orchestra and some faint daylight from the ventilators.

The darkness was audible as well as visible; for there was no mistaking that cavernous music, with the tubas lowing like Plutonian bullocks, Mime's hammer rapping weirdly, and the drums muttering the subterranean thunder of Nibelheim. And before I left the house – to be exact, it was half past twelve next morning – I actually saw Rosa Sucher and Sir Augustus Harris hand in hand before the curtain, looking as if Covent Garden had been the birthplace of her reputation, and as if he had never heard La Favorita in his life. Perhaps it was all a dream; but it seemed real to me, and does so still. Assuming that I was awake, I may claim that at least one of those curtain-calls was not for the manager at all, but for me and for those colleagues of mine who so strongly urged Sir Augustus Harris to try this experiment in the golden years when money was plenty and there was no Dissolution impending, even at the cost of depriving London of the opportunity of witnessing the début of Signor Rawner as Manrico.

The performance was vigorous, complete, earnest – in short, all that was needed to make Siegfried enormously interesting to operatic starvelings like the Covent Garden frequenters. The German orchestra is rough; but the men know the work, and are under perfect and willing discipline. In readiness and certainty of execution they are fully equal, if not superior, to the ordinary Covent Garden orchestra. But I cannot say as much for them in the matter of purity and individuality of tone. After making every allowance for the difference between the German orchestral tradition, which is partly popular, and the English, which is purely classic, as well as for the effect, peculiar to the Nibelungen tetralogy, of the rugged and massive ground bass which pervades so much of the score, I still cannot accept this imported orchestra as being up to the standard of tone quality we have been accustomed to expect in London.

In that vast mass of brass, it seemed to me that instead of three distinct and finely contrasted families of thoroughbred trombones, horns, and tubas, we had a huge tribe of mongrels, differing chiefly in size. I felt that some ancestor of the trombones had been guilty of a *mésalliance* with a bombardon; that each cornet, though itself already an admittedly half-bred trumpet, was further disgracing itself by a leaning towards the flügel horn; and that the mother of the horns must have run away with a whole military band. Something of the same doubt hangs over the lineage of the wood-wind, the bass clarionet alone being above suspicion. Even in the strings, the 'cellos and tenors lack distinction, though here the thicker and heavier tone is partly due to the lower pitch, which is in every other respect a prodigious relief. I think it will not be disputed that the Covent Garden orchestra, if it had half the opportunities of the German one, could handle the score of Siegfried not only with much greater distinction of tone and consequent variety of effect, but also with a more delicate and finished execution of the phrases which make up the mosaic of leading-motives, and with a wider range of gradation from *pianissimo* to *fortissimo* than Herr Mahler's band achieved, excellent in many respects as its performance certainly was. This is no mere conjecture: we have already heard the Siegfried blacksmith music and forest music played by our own orchestras in concert selections better than it was played on Wednesday last.

And that is why I still complain that Sir Augustus Harris is no more establishing the Wagnerian music-drama in London than Mr Kiralfy is establishing the gondola. When he organized the performance of Die Meistersinger by his own company and his own orchestra, he achieved his greatest feat as an impresario. This time he has only sent for a German impresario and a German company to help him out of the difficulty; and for that I grudge him the smallest exaltation, as I could have done as much myself if I had the requisite commercial credit.

The impression created by the performance was extraordinary, the gallery cheering wildly at the end of each act. Everybody was delighted with the change from the tailor-made operatic tenor in velvet and tights to the wild young hero who forges his own weapons and tans his own coat and buskins. We all breathed that vast orchestral atmosphere of fire, air, earth, and water, with unbounded relief and invigoration; and I doubt if half-a-dozen people in the house were troubled with the critical reflections which occurred to me whenever the orchestra took a particularly rough spin over exquisitely delicate ground, as in the scene between Wotan and Erda. It is not to be doubted that all the women found Brynhild an improvement on Carmen and Co.

I say nothing of the great drama of world-forces which the Nibelung story symbolizes, because I must not pretend that the Covent Garden performance was judged on that ground; but considering how very large a proportion of the audience was still seated when the curtain came down at half past twelve, I think it is fair to assume that the people to whom Wotan is nothing but an unmitigated bore were in a minority. At the same time, Herr Grengg, with his imposing presence, powerful voice, and perpetual fortissimo, did very little to break that ponderous monotony which is the besetting sin of the German Wotan.

Lorent, who was on the stage for a few minutes as Alberich, was also earnest, but pointless and characterless. Fortunately, Mime (Herr Lieban) saved the situation by his unflagging vivacity. It would be unreasonable to ask for a cleverer representation than his of the crafty, timid, covetous, and, one must admit, unmercifully bullied old dwarf. His singing shewed remarkable artistic ingenuity – exactly the quality which Mime's music requires.

There are two great points in the part: first, that awful nightmare which comes upon Mime after the question-and-answer scene in the first act, when he curses the shimmering light and falls into a growing terror which is just reaching an intolerable climax when it vanishes as if by magic at the voice of Siegfried in the wood outside; and, second, his attempt to poison Siegfried after the fight with the worm, when he involuntarily talks murder instead of the flattery he intends. Both of these passages were driven home forcibly by Lieban, especially the poison scene, where the effect depends more on the actor and less on the orchestra than in the other. Alvary, though he has something of that air of rather fancying himself in his part which distinguishes some of the most popular impersonations of Mr Wilson Barrett (whom Alvary rather resembles personally), attained a very considerable level of excellence as Siegfried, especially in the forest scene, the remembrance of which will, I think, prove more lasting than that of the first and last acts when we have seen a few rival Siegfrieds and grown a little more critical. Fräulein Traubmann, as the bird, was energetic, purposeful, human, and, in short, everything that a bird ought not to be. For so nice a stage illusion we need wilder and far more spontaneous woodnotes than hers.

As I have already intimated Fräulein Heink, as Erda, had her scene rather roughly handled both by the orchestra and by Wotan; but she nevertheless succeeded in rescuing something of its ineffable charm by her expressive delivery and her rich contralto tones. As to Rosa Sucher, she was as prompt, as powerful, as vigorous, as perfect in her drill, as solid and gleaming in her tone as ever. Her efficiency, brilliancy, and strength have a charm that is rather military than feminine; and consequently they will fail to rouse the voluptuous enthusiasm of our devotees of that splendid and invariably repentant female, the Womanly Woman; but as Brynhild was no Magdalen, Frau Sucher can hardly be blamed for not making her one. Finally, I have to chronicle several curtain-calls for the energetic conductor, Herr Mahler. He knows the score thoroughly, and sets the *tempi* with excellent judgment. That being so, I hope he will yet succeed in getting a finer quality of execution from his band.

The scenery is of the usual German type, majestic, but intensely prosaic. The dragon, whose vocal utterances were managed jointly by Herr Wiegand and a speaking-trumpet, was a little like Carpaccio's dragon at San Giorgio Schiavone, a little like the Temple Bar griffin, and a little like a camel about the ears, although the general foundation appeared to be an old and mangy donkey. As usual, people are complaining of the dragon as a mistake on Wagner's part, as if he were the man to have omitted a vital scene in his drama merely because our stage machinists are such duffers as to be unable, with all their resources, to make as good a dragon as I could improvise with two old umbrellas, a mackintosh, a clothes-horse, and a couple of towels. Surely it is within the scope of modern engineering to make a thing that will give its tail one smart swing round, and then rear up.

The stage effects throughout were punctual and conscientious (always excepting the flagrant exhibition of Brynhild in the last act as the Sleeping Beauty instead of as an armed figure whose sex remains a mystery until Siegfried removes the helmet and cuts away the coat of mail); but they were not very imaginative. The stithy was lighted like a Board School; and the fires of Loge and the apparition of Erda might have been ordered from the gas company, for all the pictorial art they displayed. Sir Augustus Harris need not look to Bayreuth for a lead in this direction. Where Bayreuth surpasses us is not in picturesque stage composition, but in the seriousness, punctuality, and thoroughness with which it looks after the stage business, which is mostly left to take care of itself at Covent Garden.

I am compelled by want of space to postpone until next week my notice of Mr de Lara's Light of Asia, which was successfully produced on Saturday evening. If it is repeated in the meantime, Mr de Lara will do well to withdraw the fourth act, unless the establishment can do something better in the way of staging it. It almost eclipses the absurdities of the Tannhäuser *mise en scène* at present.

Dvořák's Requiem

>><<

9 November 1892

To Dvořák's Requiem, which was performed last Wednesday at the Albert Hall, I could not be made to listen again, since the penalty of default did not exceed death; and I had much rather die than repeat the attempts I made, first at Birmingham, and then at Kensington Gore, to sit it out. It is hard to understand the frame of mind of an artist who at this time of day sits down to write a Requiem *à propos de bottes*. One can fancy an undertaker doing it readily enough: he would know as a matter of business that in music, as in joiners' work, you can take the poorest materials and set the public gaping at them by simply covering them with black cloth and coffin nails. But why should a musician condescend to speculate thus in sensationalism and superstition?

When I hear Dvořák's weird chords on muted cornets (patent Margate Pier echo attachment), finishing up with a gruesome ding on the tam-tam, I feel exactly as I should if he held up a skull with a lighted candle inside to awe me. When in the Dies Irae, he proceeds, as who should say, 'Now you shall see what I can do in the way of stage-thunder,' to turn on organ pedal and drum to make a huge mechanical modern version of the Rossini crescendo, I pointedly and publicly turn up my nose, and stare frigidly. But the public, in spite of Charles Dickens, loves everything connected with a funeral.

Those who are too respectable to stand watching the black

flag after an execution, take a creepy sort of pleasure in Requiems. If Sir Joseph Barnby were to conduct with a black brass-tipped baton; if the bandsmen wore black gloves and crape scarves; if the attendants were professional mutes (*sordini*), and the tickets edged with a half-inch jet border, I believe the enjoyment of the audience would be immensely enhanced. Dvořák seems to have felt this. Mozart's Requiem leads you away from the point: you find yourself listening to the music as music, or reflecting, or otherwise getting up to the higher planes of existence. Brahms' Requiem has not the true funeral relish: it aims at the technical traditions of requiem composition rather than the sensational, and is so execrably and ponderously dull that the very flattest of funerals would seem like a ballet, or at least a *danse macabre*, after it.

Dvořák alone, mechanically solemn and trivially genteel, very careful and elaborate in detail, and beyond belief uninspired, has hit the mean. One almost admires the perseverance with which he has cut all those dead strips of notes into length, nailed and glued them into a single structure, and titivated it for the melancholy occasion with the latest mortuary orchestral decorations. And then, the gravity with which it is received and criticized as a work of first-rate importance, as if it brought the air of a cathedral close with it, and were highly connected! Whereas, if the same music had been called 'Ode to Revolution', or 'The Apotheosis of Ibsen', or 'Dirge for the Victims of Vaccination', it would have been found out for what it is before the end of the first ten bars, as I found it out at the Birmingham Festival.

This is the way things go in England. Some few years ago Peter Benoît, a much-in-earnest Dutch composer, who is almost as great in music as Haydon was in painting, made his début here with an oratorio called Lucifer, containing one pretty song (by Schumann), but otherwise a most barren colossus of a work. The public felt that Lucifer was an integral part of the Church of England, most Englishmen being persuaded that Milton's Paradise Lost is a poetical paraphrase of the book of Genesis; and Benoît was received with deep respect as a too long neglected Dutch Beethoven. Presuming on this success, Peter laid a work called Charlotte Corday at the feet of the Philharmonic Society. That infatuated body, feeling itself traditionally committed to the discovery and encouragement of foreign Beethovens, allowed him to conduct it at one of its concerts. He promptly found out that in England, though Lucifer is respectable, Charlotte Corday is quite out of the question.

The Corday revolutionary scenes were not a whit more mechanical and shallow than the oratorio, and were nearly as bulky, besides being twice as lively (thanks to Ça ira, The Marseillaise, etc.); but the British public would have none of them; and Benoît has not since been heard of in London. I mention the matter to illustrate how easy it is to get taken seriously as a composer if you begin with an oratorio. But if you want to make assurance doubly sure, begin with a Requiem. After Dvořák every musical agent and publisher in Europe will give, as the straightest of tips to foreign composers, the word to write Requiems. I foresee the arrival of shiploads of such compositions on these coasts. When that day comes, I shall buy a broom; select some crossing out of earshot of the muffled drums; and earn my bread in a more humane and less questionably useful occupation than that which I now follow. It is true that even then I shall have to see a funeral go past occasionally. But a funeral goes past in less than two minutes, whereas a Requiem takes a matter of two hours. Besides, it is generally understood that funerals are to be avoided as long as possible, whereas Requiems are offered as a sort of treat, whether anybody is dead or not. . . .

Gluck's *Orfeo*

→>-<←

14 December 1892

I HAVE to complain strongly of the Royal College of Music for its neglect to exclude the parents and relatives of the students from its performance of Gluck's Orfeo on Saturday afternoon. The barbarous demonstrations of these Philistines, who treated the band just as they would have treated a quadrille player at one of their own dances, spoiled many a final strain in the score. Surely, if the students are to be nurtured as artists, the first and most obvious step is to cut off all communication between them and their families.

A member of an ordinary British household cannot become an artist: the thing is impossible. This was well understood in former ages with regard to the religious life, the devotees of which invariably began by cutting all their people dead, knowing full well that on no other terms was any unworldly life possible. Now the artistic life is the most unworldly of lives; and how can it be lived in any sort of association with people who, rather than wait for the band to finish Che faro senza Euridice? break into uncouth noise the moment the singer's mouth is closed?

Giulia Ravogli came to the performance, presumably to see what Gluck's Orfeo looked like. The unfamiliar spectacle must have made her envy those obscure students the artistic framework which she, one of the greatest Orfeos in the world, cannot get in the richest capital in Europe. The work was admirably put on the stage. One scene, in which a soul newly released from earth came groping into the Elysian fields, bewildered and lonely, and was discovered and welcomed by two child-shades, was a most pathetic piece of pantomime. That shade one believed to be the lost Euridice, until Euridice appeared later on in the person of quite another young lady – no great pantomimist. Very pretty, too, was the array of spirits stretching their hands after the departing Orpheus as he started on his return to earth.

The Elysian fields were situated on the uplands between Frensham and Selborne: I know the place, and thought it well chosen for the purpose. The furies and spectres were not quite up to the artistic level of the blesseder shades; and they gave no adequate sign of the shock given to them by the first note of Orpheus's lute in that dreadful region. I think, too, that the orchestral piece in D minor, since it was not danced to by the spectre, should have been played with the tableau curtain down, instead of as a storm symphony to a lightning and thunder cloth which became ridiculous after its levin bolts had remained for a couple of minutes without getting along. But the fact that these two matters exhaust my fault-finding speaks for the general excellence and artistic integrity of the staging.

The principal performer, Miss Clara Butt, a comparatively raw recruit from Bristol, far surpassed the utmost expectations that could have been reasonably entertained. She has a good voice, and went at her work without the least conceit, though with plenty of courage and originality, shewing an honesty of artistic character which is perhaps the most promising quality a novice can display. She has a rich measure of dramatic sympathy; and, considering that the management of the costume and deportment proper to the part would tax the powers of our most experienced actresses, her impersonation suffered surprisingly little from awkwardness. If Miss Butt has sufficient strength of mind to keep her eyes, ears, and mind open in the artistic atmosphere of the Royal College, without for a moment allowing herself to be taught (a process which instantly stops the alternative process of learning), she may make a considerable career for herself. . . .

The Professional Musician

→>-◄←

11 January 1893

THE Incorporated Society of Musicians has been holding its annual conference. Being rather short of subjects to confer about, it has taken to listening to music – even on the organ – to wile away the time. It is a pity we have not an incorporated society of critics, so that the musicians and critics might confer together, with a strong police force present to maintain order. It would be more amusing, even to the provincials, than organs and schools for the musical training of the blind; and the eternal question of raising the status of the musician could perhaps be met by the previous question as to what is the matter with the musician's status that he should want it raised.

It seems to me that the social opportunities of the musician are greater, instead of less, than those of other craftsmen. The church organist may find, like the rest of us, that those who pay the piper insist on calling the tune; and if they happen to have no ear and no soul for music – nay, if, as may very easily be the case, they actually make a virtue of disparaging it – the unfortunate musician may be grievously oppressed; but he is not compelled to put up with oppression because he is a musician, but solely because he depends on his post for his bread-and-butter. He is at a disadvantage, not as artist, but as employee, just as he would be in any other trade or profession. He is certainly at no social disadvantage: on the contrary, it is always assumed that the professional player of a musical instrument is socially superior to the skilled mechanic or artisan, though there is no reason in the world why he should be.

An orchestral player may be a person of distinguished culture and address; but he may also be illiterate, coarse, drunken, not scrupulously honest, and, in short, a person whom sensitive composers and conductors would not employ if his mechanical dexterity could be dispensed with. An organist may be in every respect the superior of the rector; but he is just as likely to be the inferior of the keeper of the village shop, who does not complain particularly about his status. Some of the more innocent of my readers may be shocked at this, and may demand of me whether a man whose occupation is to interpret Handel, Mozart, Beethoven, or even Jackson in B flat, is not likely to have a more elevated soul than a buyer and seller of pots and pans. I reply, not in the least. You might as well ask whether a navvy, constantly employed on vast engineering schemes, is not likely to be more large-minded than a watchmaker.

Take a man with a quick ear and quick fingers; teach him how to play an instrument and to read staff notation; give him some band practice; and there you have your 'professional', able to do what Wagner could not have done for the life of him, but no more necessarily a musician in the wider sense than a regimental marksman or broadsword instructor is necessarily a general or a master of foreign policy. He need make no more distinction between Beethoven and Brahms than a compositor does between Shakespear and Tennyson: even when he has an exceptionally fine sense of the difference between good and bad execution, he may not have the ghost of an idea of the difference between good and bad music.

Orchestral players, good enough to find constant employment in the best European orchestras, and yet with the manners, ideas, and conversation of ordinary private soldiers, are less common than formerly; but they are still contemporary facts, and not at all anomalous ones, except to muddle-headed people who imagine that every man who can play a string of notes written down by Mozart or Bach must have the heart and mind of Mozart and Bach. No doubt I shall presently be told that I have slandered an honorable profession by declaring that the members of our London orchestras are all illiterate, drunken, private-soldierly rapscallions. This is quite as near what I have just said as some of my musician-critics ever get to the meaning of my most careful and discriminate statements, let alone my more epigrammatic ones.

But the fact remains as I have stated it, that the professional musician, as such, can have no special social status whatever, because he may be anything, from an ex-drummer boy to an artist and philosopher of world-wide reputation. It would be far more reasonable to demand a special status for the musical critic as such, since he is bound to be skilled in music, in literature, and in criticism, which no man can be without a far wider culture than an executive musician need possess. But I never have any trouble about my status, though I probably should have if I were asked to draw the line between myself and the country-town reporter who occasionally copies out a concert program and prefaces it with a few commonplaces. I am welcome among the people who like my ways and manners; and I believe musicians enjoy the same advantage.

When we are not welcome, probably the ways and manners are to blame, and not the profession.

With this soothing contribution to the ever-burning question of the conference, I pass on to the part of it which I personally attended: to wit, the lecture on the spinet, harpsichord, and clavichord by Mr Hipkins, and that on the lute and viols by Mr Arnold Dolmetsch. ...

Music Criticism

→>—<←

15 February 1893

I do not know how far the matter is worth mentioning, but music is dying out in London. The Monday Popular and Ballad concerts go on from mere force of habit; the Crystal Palace concerts will begin again next Saturday, because they rashly promised to do so last year; oratorios are solemnized at the usual intervals in the Albert Hall; Sarasate goes and Joachim comes; and Mr Henschel's band is heard twice a month as usual. It is true that early February is not exactly the height of the musical season, and that this year the light-opera-houses produced their novelties much earlier in the year than is customary.

But when all allowances are made, it must be admitted that things for the moment are slack; and I have once or twice thought of raising an Unemployed Deadheads' agitation, and calling on the Government to at once set on foot a series of Relief Concerts, at which these unhappy people may pass their afternoons and evenings. The Abolition of Piece-work for critics would be a prominent plank in the program of such an agitation; for even a critic must live, and if the agents will not give concerts and recitals, the critics will be driven to invent them; that is the long and short of it.

A man cannot go on repeating what he has said a thousand times about the way the Monday Popular quartet played Haydn in G, No. 12 of Opus 756, or about Santley as Elijah. I turn in desperation to the musical journals, and my hopes rise as I see the words 'Ignorant Misstatement'. But it is actually not G. B. S. this time; somebody else, I suppose, has made a remark sufficiently obvious to shake the foundation of make-believe on which 'art' of the usual professional type is built. The tenants of that fashionable edifice are always protesting that I am an impudent pretender to musical authority, betraying my ignorance, in spite of my diabolical cunning, in every second sentence. And I do not mind confessing that I do not know half as much as you would suppose from my articles; but in the kingdom of the deaf the one-eared is king.

The other evening I was looking into a shop-window in Oxford Street, when a gentleman accosted me modestly, and, after flattering me with great taste and modesty into an entire willingness to make his acquaintance, began with evident misgiving and hesitation, but with no less evident curiosity, to approach the subject of these columns. At last he came to his point with a rush by desperately risking the question, 'Excuse me, Mr G. B. S., but *do* you know anything about music? The fact is, I am not capable of forming an opinion myself; but Dr Blank says you don't, and – er – Dr Blank is such a great authority that one hardly knows what to think.' Now this question put me into a difficulty, because I had already learnt by experience that the reason my writings on music and musicians are so highly appreciated is, that they are supposed by many of my greatest admirers to be a huge joke, the point of which lies in the fact that I am totally ignorant of music, and that my character of critic is an exquisitely ingenious piece of acting, undertaken to gratify my love of mystification and paradox.

From this point of view every one of my articles appears as a fine stroke of comedy, occasionally broadening into a harlequinade, in which I am the clown, and Dr Blank the policeman. At first I did not realize this, and could not understand the air of utter disillusion and loss of interest in me that would come over people in whose houses I incautiously betrayed some scrap of amateurish enlightenment. But the naïve exclamation, 'Oh! you *do* know something about it, then,' at last became familiar to me; and I now take particular care not to expose my knowledge. When people hand me a sheet of instrumental music, and ask my opinion of it, I carefully hold it upside down, and pretend to study it in that position with the eye of an expert. When they invite me to try their new grand piano, I attempt to open it at the wrong end; and when the young lady of the house informs me that she is practising the 'cello, I innocently ask her whether the mouthpiece did not cut her lips dreadfully at first. This line of conduct gives enormous satisfaction, in which I share to a rather greater extent than is generally supposed. But, after all, the people whom I take in thus are only amateurs.

To place my impostorship beyond question I require to be certified as such by authorities like our Bachelors and Doctors of music – gentlemen who can write a Nunc Dimittis in five real parts, and know the difference between a tonal fugue and a real one, and can tell you how old Monteverde was on his thirtieth birthday, and have views as to the true root of the discord of the seventh on the supertonic, and devoutly believe that *si contra fa diabolus est*. But I have only to present myself to them in the character of a man who has been through these dreary games without ever discovering the remotest vital connection between them and the art of music – a state of mind so inconceivable by them – to make them exclaim:

> Preposterous ass! that never read so far
> To know the cause why music was ordained,

and give me the desired testimonials at once. And so I manage to scrape along without falling under suspicion of being an honest man.

However, since mystification is not likely to advance us in the long run, may I suggest that there must be something wrong in the professional tests which have been successively applied to Handel, to Mozart, to Beethoven, to Wagner, and last, though not least, to me, with the result in every case of our condemnation as ignoramuses and charlatans. Why is it that when Dr Blank writes about music nobody but a professional musician can understand him; whereas the man-in-the-street, if fond of art and capable of music, can understand the writings of Mendelssohn, Wagner, Liszt, Berlioz, or any of the composers?

Why, again, is it that my colleague, W. A., for instance, in criticizing Mr Henry Arthur Jones's play the other day, did not *parse* all the leading sentences in it? I will not be so merciless as to answer these questions now, though I know the solution, and am capable of giving it if provoked beyond endurance. Let it suffice for the moment that writing is a very difficult art, criticism a very difficult process, and music not easily to be distinguished, without special critical training, from the scientific, technical, and professional conditions of its performance, composition, and teaching. And if the critic is to please the congregation, who want to read only about the music, it is plain that he must appear quite beside the point to the organ-blower, who wants to read about his bellows, which he can prove to be the true source of all the harmony. . . .

Beethoven's Choral Symphony

→→⊷←←

8 March 1893

A PERFORMANCE of the Ninth Symphony always brings a special audience to St James's Hall; for it is known to be the masterpiece of modern tone poetry, and the literary man comes to complete his culture by listening to it. I always pity him as he sits there, bothered and exhausted, wondering how soon the choir will begin to sing those verses which are the only part of the analytic program of which he can make head or tail, and hardly able to believe that the conductor can be serious in keeping the band moodling on for forty-five mortal minutes before the singers get to business. Time was when the conductor himself was often still more astray than the literary man as to the intention of Beethoven, and when those who knew the work by heart sat snorting in contemptuous rage, or enduring with the habitual resignation of tamed despair, whilst the dreary ceremony of reading through the band parts was proceeding.

When I say 'time *was*', I do not for a moment question the ability of London to reproduce the same discouraging results still: no doubt anyone who may be curious to know exactly what I mean will find sufficient opportunity before we have lost all the traditions of the time when the Ninth Symphony was treated exactly as if it were a quintet for pianoforte, flute, etc., by Hummel, re-scored for full orchestra by Beethoven. But it has now become a matter of tolerably common knowledge that this sort of handling stamps a conductor, not as a leading authority on Beethoven, but as a nincompoop. How far the work has become really popular it would be hard to determine, because, as I have said, so many people come whenever it is in the bills, not to enjoy themselves, but to improve themselves. To them the culmination of its boredom in an Ode to Joy must seem a wanton mockery, since they always hear it for the first time; for a man does not sacrifice himself in that way twice, just as he does not read Daniel Deronda twice; and consequently, since it is pre-eminently true of the Ninth Symphony as of the hero of the music-hall song, that it is all right when you know it but you've got to know it first, he never becomes sufficiently familiar with the work to delight in it.

On the other hand, there must be a growing number of persons who, like myself, would rather have the Ninth Symphony, even from the purely musical point of view, than all the other eight put together, and to whom, besides, it is religious music, and its performance a celebration rather than an entertainment. I am highly susceptible to the force of all truly religious music, no matter to what Church it belongs; but the music of my own Church – for which I may be allowed, like other people, to have a partiality – is to be found in the Die Zauberflöte and the Ninth Symphony. I was born into evil days, when Les Huguenots was considered a sublime creation, and Die Zauberflöte 'a damned pantomime' (as they say nowadays of its legitimate successor, Das Rheingold), and when the Ninth Symphony was regarded as a too long and perversely ugly and difficult concert-piece, much inferior to such august neo-classics as Spohr's Consecration of Sound and Mendelssohn's Italian Symphony; and if I had won all my knowledge of the great Singspiel and the great Symphony from their interpreters, instead of from Mozart and Beethoven themselves, small and darkened would that knowledge have been.

In bygone days I have often sat at performances, and said, under my breath, to the conductor or the artists, 'Ah! if I were only a musical critic, how I would pay you out for this, you impostor, you pedant, you miserable artistic deaf-mute, you bawling upstart, you conceited minx,' etc., etc., etc. That was in the day of my hot youth. Fortunately, I never became a professed critic – to my own great surprise – until age and experience had softened me to my present indulgent mellowness; but I am by nature vindictive, and find myself not always proof against the temptation to pay off old scores against hardened sinners; so that sometimes, when a fellow-creature is catching it in this column ostensibly for some shortcoming in the previous week, he (or she) is really expiating some murderous art-outrage perpetrated on a defenceless child a quarter of a century ago – perhaps even – and this, I admit, is the climax of injustice – by somebody else of whom the performance has too vividly reminded me.

Therefore I implore all young artists to do their best under all circumstances; for they can never know who is listening to them, or how soon some insignificant brat in the cheap seats in a provincial Town Hall or Athenaeum may rise up, an avenging fury, armed with all the terrors of the London Press.

As to Mr Henschel and his performance of the Ninth Symphony last Thursday, when I say that he quite understood the nature of the work, and was not for a moment in danger of the old fundamental error of treating it as mere musical arabesque, I imply that the performance was a success; for, with a good band and a right understanding, the obscurities and difficulties of the Ninth Symphony vanish, and a child may lead it. The concert began with Schubert's unfinished symphony, which on this occasion ought to have been his uncommenced symphony. The Ninth Symphony is quite enough for one evening; and I purposely came late for the first movement of the Schubert part of the program, and did not listen to the second. When we got to Beethoven our minds were soon set at ease as to Mr Henschel's grasp of the situation by the vigor and decision with which we got the first subject, especially those two final bars with which

Beethoven so powerfully clinches it. But though the main point was thus secured, the handling of the movement as it proceeded was not by any means above criticism.

Mr Henschel, like Ibsen's Master Builder, and like all good conductors, has a troll in him; and this troll occasionally takes to rampaging and filibustering, at which seasons Mr Henschel will not only tolerate, and even relish, rough and blatant attacks on imposing passages, but will overdrive his band in a manner recalling some of the most remarkable achievements of Bevignani. Now, Beethoven must have known well that this was one of the common faults of the qualities he required in a conductor; and it seems clear to me that it was his dread lest any vulgar urgency or excitement should mar the grandeur of his symphonic masterpiece that led him to give the *tempo* of the first movement not merely as *allegro*, but as '*allegro*, but not too much so – rather majestically'. Mr Henschel certainly missed the full significance of this 'un poco maestoso'. He made more than one undignified spurt; and at each of these incontinences the execution became blurred and confused, even to the point, if I mistake not, of notes being dropped and hasty recoveries made in the next bar by the wood-wind.

In the Scherzo, which lends itself to impetuous treatment, the *tempo* was perfect, varying between a normal hundred and seventeen bars per minute and an exceptional hundred and twenty. There were many admirable points in the execution of the slow movement, notably the cantabile of the second violins in the first of the andante sections; and the only matter on which I found myself at odds with the conductor was the concluding twelve-eight section, where the fact, hardly noticeable at first in the common time, that the pace was a shade too fast for a true Beethoven adagio, become quite obvious. Later on, Mr Henschel rather astonished some of us by the apparently very slow *tempo* he adopted for the *allegro assai*, in which the basses give out the theme of the Ode to Joy. We are so accustomed to hear this played exactly twice too fast, as if the minims and crotchets were quavers and semiquavers, and treated as a Haydn allegro instead of as an expressive melody, that some of the older listeners felt a little indignant with Mr Henschel for not taking the usual wrong course.

I will even confess that I myself think that the thirty-three bars per minute, increasing to thirty-six at the *forte*, might have been changed to thirty-six and forty respectively without any worse effect than the correction of a slight failing that leaned to virtue's side. The choral portion was perhaps as well done as was possible under the circumstances at English concert pitch; but the strain was inhuman; and the florid variation beat both the choir and the principals, since it required smooth vocal execution as well as mere pluck, which quality the choir shewed abundantly as they held on desperately to high A after high A. On the whole, if we cannot get the pitch down, I am prepared to face the transposition of the choral section a semitone rather than have it marred by tearing and straining at impossibilities. The best points in the vocal work were the charming *piano* on the lines Who can not, oh let him, weeping, Steal away and live alone; the great chorus, Oh! embrace now all ye millions, and the martial tenor solo, which was sung with intelligence and spirit by Mr Henry McKinley.

May I suggest, on behalf of the choir, that if their voices are not to be relieved by the introduction of French pitch, at least their lungs might be refreshed by the introduction of a little fresh air? My enjoyment of the symphony was considerably interfered with by the background of young women, beauteous in their virgin robes, but visibly stifling, and agitating fans and sheets of music in all sorts of contradictory rhythms. At last, just as the exquisite coda of the adagio was stealing on me, I happened to catch sight of a face which had gone perfectly white; and then, of course, I gave up the adagio with a sigh, and resigned myself to watch the progress of the struggle not to faint and disturb the performance, the conviction that fresh air was the only salvation, the dreadful sense of the impossibility of climbing to the door over those giddy seats with the lights whirling round and the ground reeling, the alarm spreading to the neighbors, the proffering of fans and smelling-bottles, the commotion among gallant tenors and basses at the back, and the final desperate rally of the patient, and her triumphant postponement of her collapse to the top of the steep ladder at the other side of the door. During all which the band might have been playing Pop Goes the Weasel with no more fear of detection than if we had all been a St John's Ambulance class. . . .

Falstaff

12 April 1893

EASTER has afforded me an opportunity for a look through the vocal score of Verdi's Falstaff, now to be had at Ricordi's for sixteen shillings, a price which must obviously be reduced before the opera can get into the hands of the amateur at large. I did not go to Milan to hear the first performance for several reasons, the chief being that I am not enough of a first-nighter to face the huge tedium and probable sickness of the journey from Holborn to Basle (the rest I do not mind) in order merely to knock at the tradesman's door of Italy, so to speak, and turn back after hearing an opera half murdered by La Scala prima donnas with shattering tremolos, and witnessing a Grand Old Man demonstration conducted for the most part by people who know about as much of music as the average worshipper of Mr Gladstone does of statesmanship. In short, being lazy and heavily preoccupied, I cried sour grapes and stayed at home, knowing that the mountain would come to Mahomet soon enough.

Let it be understood, then, that since I have not been present at a complete performance of Falstaff I do not know the work: I only know some things about it. And of these I need not repeat what has already been sufficiently told: as, for instance, that Falstaff is a music drama, not an opera, and that consequently it is by Shakespear, Boito, and Verdi, and not by Verdi alone. The fact that it is a music drama explains the whole mystery of its composition by a man eighty years old. If there were another Il balen or La donna è mobile in it, I should have been greatly astonished; but there is nothing of the sort: the fire and heroism of his earlier works blazes up now only on strong provocation.

Falstaff is lighted and warmed only by the afterglow of the fierce noonday sun of Ernani; but the gain in beauty conceals the loss in heat – if, indeed, it be a loss to replace intensity of passion and spontaneity of song by fullness of insight and perfect mastery of workmanship. Verdi has exchanged the excess of his qualities for the wisdom to supply his deficiencies; his weaknesses have disappeared with his superfluous force; and he is now, in his dignified competence, the greatest of living dramatic composers. It is not often that a man's strength is so immense that he can remain an athlete after bartering half of it to old age for experience; but the thing happens occasionally, and need not so greatly surprise us in Verdi's case, especially those of us who, long ago, when Von Bülow and others were contemptuously repudiating him, were able to discern in him a man possessing more power than he knew how to use, or indeed was permitted to use, by the old operatic forms imposed on him by circumstances.

I have noticed one or two exclamations of surprise at the supposed revelation in Falstaff of a 'hitherto unsuspected' humorous force in the veteran tragic composer. This must be the result of the enormous popularity which Il Trovatore first and Aida afterwards attained in this country. I grant that these operas are quite guiltless of comic relief; but what about Un Ballo, with its exquisitely light-hearted E scherz' od è follia, and the finale to the third act, where Renato is sarcastically complimented on his domestic virtue by the conspirators who have just shewn him that the Duke's veiled mistress, whom he is defending from them after devotedly saving the Duke's life, is his own wife. Stupidly as that tragi-comic quartet and chorus has always been mishandled on our wretched operatic stage, I cannot understand anyone who knows it denying Verdi's gift of dramatic humor.

In the first act of Otello, the stretto made in the drinking song by Cassio when he gets drunk is very funny without being in the least unmusical. The grim humor of Sparafucile, the terrible ironic humor of Iago, the agonized humor of Rigoletto: these surely settled the question as to Verdi's capacity for Falstaff none the less because the works in which they occur are tragedies and not comedies. All that could be said on the other side was that Verdi was no Mozart, which was as idle as saying that Victor Hugo was no Molière. Verdi's vein of humor is all the more Shakespearean on that account.

Verdi's worst sins as a composer have been sins against the human voice. His habit of taking the upper fifth of the compass of an exceptionally high voice, and treating that fifth as the normal range, has a great deal to do with the fact that the Italian singer is now the worst singer in the world, just as Wagner's return to Handel's way of using the voice all over its compass and obtaining physical relief for the singer and artistic relief for the audience by the contrast of the upper and lower registers has made the Wagnerian singer now the best singer in the world. Verdi applied his system with special severity to baritones.

If you look at the score of Don Giovanni, you will find three different male voices written for on the bass clef, and so treated as to leave no doubt that Mozart, as he wrote the music, had a particular sort of voice for each part constantly in his head, and that one (Masetto's) was a rough peasant's bass, another (Leporello's) a ready, fluent, copious *basso cantante*; and the third a light fine baritone, the voice of a gentleman. I have heard public meetings addressed successively by an agricultural laborer's delegate, a representative of the skilled artisans, and a university man; and they have taught me what all the treatises on singing in the world could not about the Mozartian differentiation between Masetto, Leporello, and Don Giovanni.

But now please remark that there is no difference of range between the three parts. Any man who can sing the notes of one of them can sing the notes of the others. Let Masetto and the Don exchange characters, and though the Don will be utterly ineffective in the concerted music on Masetto's lower G's and B flats, whilst Masetto will rob the serenade of all its delicacy, yet neither singer will encounter any more impossibility, or even inconvenience, in singing the notes than Mr Toole would have in reading the part of Hamlet. The same thing is true of the parts of Bartolo, Figaro, and Almaviva in Le Nozze; of San Bris and Nevers in Les Huguenots; of Wotan and Alberich in The Niblung's Ring; and of Amfortas and Klingsor in Parsifal. The dramatic distinction between these parts is so strong that only an artist of remarkable versatility could play one as well as the other; but there is practically no distinction of vocal range any more than there is a distinction of physical stature or strength.

But if we turn to Il Trovatore, we find two vocal parts written in the bass clef, of which the lower, Ferrando, is not a *basso profondo* like Osmin or Marcel, but a *basso cantante* like San Bris or Leporello; yet the baritone part (Di Luna) is beyond the reach of any normal *basso cantante*, and treats a baritone voice as consisting of about one effective octave, from G on the fourth space of the bass stave to the G above. In Il balen there are from two hundred and ten to two hundred and twenty notes, including the cadenza, etc. Barring five notes in the cadenza, which is never sung as written, only three are below F on the fourth line, whilst nearly one hundred and forty lie above the stave between B flat and the high G. The singing is practically continuous from end to end; and the strain on a normal baritone voice is frightful, even when the song is transposed half a tone as it usually is to bring it within the bare limits of possibility. Di Luna is in this respect a typical Verdi baritone; and the result has been that only singers with abnormally high voices have been able to sing it without effort.

As to the normal baritones who have made a specialty of bawling fiercely up to G sharp, they have so lost the power of producing an endurable tone in their lower octave, or of pitching its notes with even approximate accuracy, that they have all but destroyed the popularity of Mozart's operas by their occasional appearances as Don Giovanni, Figaro, etc. I have often wished that the law would permit me to destroy these unhappy wretches, whose lives must be a burden to them. It is easy to go into raptures over the superiority of the Italian master in vocal writing because his phrases are melodious, easily learned, symmetrical, and often grandiose; but when you have to sing the melodious well-turned phrases, and find that they lie a tone higher than you can comfortably manage them, and a third higher than you can keep on managing them for five minutes at a stretch (for music that *lies* rather high is much more trying than music that *ventures* very high occasionally), you begin to appreciate the sort of knowledge of and consideration for the voice shewn by Purcell, Handel, and Wagner, and to very decidedly resent Verdi's mere partiality for the top end of it.

Now comes the question, what sort of voice is needed for the part of Falstaff? Well, Ferrando and the Count di Luna rolled into one – Amonasro, in short. A rich *basso cantante*, who can knock out a vigorous high G and play with F sharp as Melba plays with B flat. Polyphemus in Handel's Acis and Valentine in Gounod's Faust might do it justice between them. Barely reasonable this, even at French pitch, and monstrous at Philharmonic pitch. And yet it is the fashion to say that Verdi is a master of the art of writing singable music.

The score is necessarily occupied to a great extent by the discourses of Falstaff, which are set with the most expert ingenuity and subtlety, the advance in this respect from the declamation of Charles V in Ernani to that of Falstaff being as great as from Tannhäuser's to Parsifal's, or from Vanderdecken's to Hans Sachs's. One capital effect – the negative answers in the manner of Mr Chadband to the repeated questions as to what honor is – is, musically, a happy adaptation from Boito's Mefistofele, and is, as far as I have discovered, the only direct Boitoism in the work, though I imagine that Verdi has profited generally by having so fine an artist and critic as Boito at his elbow when composing Otello and Falstaff. There are some amusing passages of instrumental music: for instance, a highly expressive accompaniment to a colossal drink taken by Falstaff.

During the abundant action and stage bustle of the piece we get a symphonic treatment, which belongs exclusively to Verdi's latest manner. Some tripping figuration, which creates perpetual motion by its ceaseless repetition in all sorts of ingenious sequences, as in Mendelssohn's scherzos or the finales to his concertos, is taken as the musical groundwork upon which the vocal parts are put in, the whole fabric being wrought with the most skilful elegance. This is a matter for some of our musical pundits to consider rather anxiously. For, if I had said ten years ago that Ernani was a much greater musical composition than Mendelssohn's Scotch symphony or any of his concertos, words could not have conveyed the scorn with which so gross an opinion would have been received. But here, today, is the scorned one, whom even Browning thought it safe to represent as an empty blusterer shrinking amid a torrent of vulgar applause from the grave eye of – of – of – well, of ROSSINI! (poor Browning!) falling back in his old age on the Mendelssohnian method, and employing it with ease and brilliancy.

Perhaps, when Verdi turns a hundred and feels too old for opera composition, he will take to concerto writing, and cut out Mendelssohn and Schumann in the pretty pattern work which the pundits love them for. Which will shew how very easy it is for a good musician, when he happens to be a bad critic, to admire a great composer for the wrong thing.

Amateur Concert at Richmond

+>-<+

26 April 1893

IN the eye of an inconsiderate public, concerts given by amateur orchestral societies hardly seem worth the serious attention of a critic who is busy watching the symptoms of the Philharmonic, the Crystal Palace, the London Symphony, the Richter, and the Hallé orchestras. Yet to me the amateur orchestra is all-important; for out of every ten people who support music in England, at least nine and three-quarters must have acquired their knowledge of it as amateurs and from amateurs. The musician of professional antecedents is an incorrigible deadhead: whether he performs or listens, music has to support him, instead of being supported by him.

It is clear that a man cannot cultivate a taste for orchestral music by listening once a week to a church service accompanied by the combination of pan-pipes and accordion which has replaced the old-fashioned village church band, or even by occasionally patronizing a travelling dramatic company in the town-hall, and studying the efforts of a pianist, backed by three fiddles and a cornet, to give a satisfactory account of the overture to William Tell, Mascagni's intermezzo, and a twenty-year-old waltz by Waldteufel. The moment you step outside the circle of London, Birmingham, Manchester, Bristol, Glasgow, and towns of their calibre, you have to choose between amateur music and no music at all; whilst even in these big towns music is really kept alive by professional musicians who as teachers discover amateur talent, and as conductors and concert-givers organize it for the performance of the masterpieces of modern music.

The professional orchestral conductor who is a conductor and nothing else, and who conducts professional singers and players exclusively, only exists in great capitals. It takes London and Vienna combined to keep Richter in this position, and Glasgow and the Crystal Palace combined to keep Manns in it; and both these eminent conductors have to depend on amateurs for the performance of choral works. Had Destiny buried them in a small provincial town, they would, whilst they remained there, have had to put up with an amateur band, and amateur principal singers into the bargain. And there are suburbs of London which are in darkness more deplorable than any country town.

Under these circumstances, it seems to me that the critic who considers an amateur orchestra beneath his notice stamps himself as a hopeless Cockney – that is, a man who does not know the country because he has never lived there, and does not know London because he has never lived anywhere else. Last week Mr James Brown, the conductor of the Richmond Orchestral Society, had the gumption to surmise that a stroll out to Richmond Hill to hear what his Society can do might seem to me at least as tempting a way of spending an evening as a visit to Steinway or Prince's Hall to hear the annual concert of Miss Smith or Miss Brown, aided by more or less distinguished artists singing exactly what they have sung on similar occasions for a whole generation of miscellaneous concerts. I accepted his invitation, and arrived at sundown on the terrace, where I mused over the site of that Wagner Theatre which yet remains unbuilt, until it was time to go into the 'Star and Garter' and get to business.

The program was of the usual amateur kind: that is to say, it would have taxed the finest qualities of the best band in the world. Mozart's G Minor symphony, the Lohengrin prelude, Mendelssohn's Athalie overture and his violin concerto: only such works as these can inspire the mighty craving and dogged perseverance which carry a man through that forlorn hope, the making of an orchestra out of nothing. When you start you are received with enthusiasm by men who can play the posthorn, the banjo, the concertina, and every other instrument not used in the orchestra. You enlist trombone-players only to find that though they can 'vamp' they cannot read, and propose to assist you by improvising a bass continuously to whatever may be going on. You can choose the two least execrable out of twenty cornet-players at the cost of making eighteen bitter enemies in the neighborhood; but you are lucky if you find one horn-player, although you require four. Flutes, too, are comparatively plentiful; whilst clarionets are scarce, oboes all but unknown, and bassoons quite out of the question (though there is a lady-bassoonist at Richmond).

In the string department the same difficulty arises. Young ladies who can play much better than the average professional 'leader' of twenty years ago are discoverable with a little research in sufficient abundance nowadays (chiefly because Madame Neruda proved at that time that the violin shews off a good figure); and the violoncello, for some less obvious reason, fascinates tiny women sufficiently to keep itself fairly alive in amateur circles. But nobody will touch the double bass; and the viola comes to grief almost as signally as it used to do in the professional band in the old days, when only worn-out violinists scraped the tenor, and when such viola parts as those in Tristan or Harold, and such players as Hollander condescending to the instrument, were unknown.

When trying to get an orchestra together the conductor stops at nothing, except at houses whence come sounds of practising on an orchestral instrument. I have known a man, on catching this doleful noise at midnight on his way home from rehearsal, listen at the area-railings, take a note of the address, and call next day to kidnap the practiser by reckless flatteries. I have known valuable appointments, involving the transfer of learned professors from the Metropolis to provincial towns, decided by the frantic efforts of a local conductor to secure the election of a candidate who was said to be a proficient player on one of the scarcer instruments. But it is when the orchestra is actually formed and set to work that its creator tastes the full bitterness of his position.

The unredeemed villainy of the amateur nature is not easy to describe adequately. Its outrageous frivolity, to which no engagement is sacred, and its incredible vanity, to which art is nothing and the lower self everything, baffle my powers of description, and make me for once regret that I do not wield one of those bitter, biting pens which were made to lash offenders on whom mercy is thrown away – for instance, those two amateur extremes, the man who never attends a rehearsal but always turns up at the concert, and the man who attends all the rehearsals and blenches from the concert. Even your leader will miss a rehearsal to go to a dance, or will coolly tell you on the morning of the concert that he cannot play because his father is dead, or some such frivolous excuse. Then there is the incompetent wind-player who has a bit of solo which he cannot execute, and who, at the last moment, must have his part doubled by a professional to save public disgrace and breakdown.

On such occasions the professional, regarding all amateurs as blacklegs, is offensive; objects to having his part doubled; says, 'Look here! Who's going to play this – me or you?' etc., etc. The amateur sulks, broods over his injuries, leaves the orchestra, and probably tries to establish a rival society for the performance of wind-instrument chamber-music. The difficulties are endless, and the artistic results agonizing, since the progress made by the people who stick to the rehearsals is always spoiled at the last moment by the backwardness of those who dont.

I will not pretend that the concert at Richmond did not bear the marks of these hard conditions. It began short-handed, especially in the horn department. At the end of the overture a gentleman in irreproachable evening-dress, smiling, and carrying a black bag presenting the general outline of a French-horn, appeared and climbed up on the platform with a sort of 'Here I am, you see, safe and sound – never say die' air about him. As he mounted there was a crash of breaking wood, from which I gathered that he had succeeded in completing the sensation by shattering the platform. The conductor received him with grim patience, concealing all signs of the murderous thoughts that must have raged within him. Just imagine Mr Borsdorf, for instance, playing that trick on Richter! I wonder did it occur to the gentleman that money had been obtained from the public, with his consent, on the strength of his being in his place to play one of the horn parts in the overture. If it is too much to expect an ordinary English gentleman to be artistically conscientious, surely we may at least call on him to be commercially honest. However, justice forbids me to urge too harshly the offence of the man who came in after the overture, since I must perforce say nothing of the worse offenders who did not come at all. Almost immediately after the beginning of the Lohengrin prelude the band divided itself into two resolute factions, one maintaining that the bar in hand was the sixth bar, and the other equally convinced that it was the seventh. So they agreed to differ; and I listened with a drunken sensation of hearing the prelude double until the wind instruments rushed into the fray, and, mostly taking the side which the conductor had supported from the first, made the opposition waver and finally come over one by one, the fortissimo being played with almost entire unanimity. In the accompaniment to O star of eve! (Tannhäuser) the tremolando to the words Da scheinest du, etc., was ruined by the shirking of some lady-violinists, who, with faces expressive of the most shameful irresolution, and fear of being heard, rested their bows helplessly on the strings and sat quivering – an exceedingly amateur way of tremolandoing. But in spite of these and similar mishaps, I felt throughout that the thing was well worth doing. . . .

Stanford's 'Irish' Symphony

>-<

10 May 1893

THE success of Professor Stanford's Irish Symphony last Thursday was, from the Philharmonic point of view, somewhat scandalous. The spectacle of a university professor 'going Fantee' is indecorous, though to me personally it is delightful. When Professor Stanford is genteel, cultured, classic, pious, and experimentally mixolydian, he is dull beyond belief. His dullness is all the harder to bear because it is the restless, ingenious, trifling, flippant dullness of the Irishman, instead of the stupid, bovine, sleepable-through dullness of the Englishman, or even the aggressive, ambitious, sentimental dullness of the Scot. But Mr Villiers Stanford cannot be dismissed as merely the Irish variety of the professional species.

Take any of the British oratorios and cantatas which have been produced recently for the Festivals, and your single comment on any of them will be – if you know anything about music – 'Oh! anybody with a bachelor's degree could have written that.' But you cannot say this of Stanford's Eden. It is as insufferable a composition as any Festival committee could desire; but it is ingenious and peculiar; and although in it you see the Irish professor trifling in a world of ideas, in marked contrast to the English professor conscientiously wrestling in a vacuum, yet over and above this national difference, which would assert itself equally in the case of any other Irishman, you find certain traces of a talent for composition, which is precisely what the ordinary professor, with all his grammatical and historical accomplishments, utterly lacks. But the conditions of making this talent serviceable are not supplied by Festival commissions. Far from being a respectable oratorio-manufacturing talent, it is, when it gets loose, eccentric, violent, romantic, patriotic, and held in check only by a mortal fear of being found deficient in what are called 'the manners and tone of good society'. This fear, too, is Irish: it is, possibly, the racial consciousness of having missed that four hundred years of Roman civilization which gave England a sort of university education when Ireland was in the hedge school.

In those periods when nobody questions the superiority of the university to the hedge school, the Irishman, lamed by a sense of inferiority, blusters most intolerably, and not unfrequently goes the length of alleging that Balfe was a great composer. Then the fashion changes; Ruskin leads young Oxford out into the hedge school to dig roads; there is general disparagement in advanced circles of civilization, the university, respectability, law and order; and a heroic renunciation of worldly and artificial things is insisted upon by those who, having had their fling, are tired of them, a demand powerfully reinforced by the multitude, who want to have their fling but cannot get it under existing circumstances, and are driven to console themselves by crying sour grapes.

This reaction is the opportunity of the Irishman in England to rehabilitate his self-respect, since it gives him a standpoint from which he can value himself as a hedge-school man, patron-ize the university product, and escape from the dreary and abor-tive task of branding himself all over as an Irish snob under the impression that he is hallmarking himself as an English gentle-man. If he seizes the opportunity, he may end in founding a race of cultivated Irishmen whose mission in England will be to teach Englishmen to play with their brains as well as with their bodies; for it is all work and no play in the brain department that makes John Bull such an uncommonly dull boy.

The beginning of this 'return to nature' in music has been effected, not by a sudden repudiation of the whole academic system, but by the smuggling into academic music of ancient folk-music under various pretences as to its archaeological im-portance; its real recommendation, of course, being that the musicians like the tunes, and the critics and programists find it much easier to write about 'national characteristics' and 'the interval of the augmented second' than to write to the point. First we had Mendelssohn's 'Scotch' Symphony, and then came a deluge of pseudo-Hungarian, gipsy, and other folk-music – Liszt, Bruch, Dvořák, and Brahms all trying their hands – with, in due course, 'pibrochs' by Dr Mackenzie, Land of the Mountain and the Flood overture from Mr Hamish MacCunn, and Villiers Stanford's Irish Symphony. No general criticism of the works produced in this movement is possible.

The poorer composers, unable to invent interesting themes for their works in sonata form, gladly availed themselves of the licence to steal popular airs, with results that left them as far as ever behind the geniuses who assimilated what served their turn in folk-music as in every other store of music. But, at all events, the new fashion produced music quite different in kind from the Turkish music devised by the German Mozart for Il Seraglio, the Arabian music copied by his countryman Weber for Oberon, or the African and Scotch music invented by Mendelssohn and Meyerbeer (both Jews) for L'Africaine and the Scotch Symphony. This sort of 'national' music takes the artificial operatic or sonata forms quite easily, submitting to be soaped and washed and toiletted for its visit to Covent Garden or St James's Hall without the least awkwardness.

But in the recent cases where the so-called folk-music is written by a composer born of the folk himself, and especially of the Celtic folk, with its intense national sentiment, there is the most violent repugnance between the popular music and the sonata form. The 'Irish' Symphony, composed by an Irishman, is a record of fearful conflict between the aboriginal Celt and the Professor. The scherzo is not a scherzo at all, but a shindy, expending its force in riotous dancing. However hopelessly an English orchestra may fail to catch the wild nuances of the Irish fiddler, it cannot altogether drown the 'hurroosh' with which Stanford the Celt drags Stanford the Professor into the orgy. Again, in the slow movement the emotional development is such as would not be possible in an English or German symphony. At first it is slow, plaintive, passionately sad about nothing.

According to all classic precedent, it should end in hopeless gloom, in healing resignation, or in pathetic sentiment. What it does end in is blue murder, the Professor this time aiding and abetting the transition with all his contrapuntal might. In the last movement the rival Stanfords agree to a compromise which does not work. The essence of the sonata form is the development of themes; and even in a rondo a theme that will not develop will not fit the form. Now the greatest folk-songs are final developments themselves: they cannot be carried any further. You cannot develop God Save the Queen, though you may, like Beethoven, write some interesting but retrograde variations on it. Neither can you develop Let Erin remember. You might, of course, develop it inversely, debasing it touch by touch until you had The Marseillaise in all its vulgarity; and the doing of this might be instructive, though it would not be symphony writing. But no forward development is possible.

Yet in the last movement of the Irish Symphony, Stanford the Celt, wishing to rejoice in Molly Macalpine (Remember the glories) and The Red Fox (Let Erin remember), insisted that if Stanford the Professor wanted to develop themes, he should develop these two. The Professor succumbed to the shillelagh of his double, but finding development impossible, got out of the difficulty by breaking Molly up into fragments, exhibiting these fantastically, and then putting them together again. This process is not in the least like the true sonata development. It would not work at all with The Red Fox, which comes in as a flagrant patch upon the rondo – for the perfect tune that is one moment a war song, and the next, without the alteration of a single note, the saddest of patriotic reveries 'on Lough Neagh's bank where the fisherman strays in the clear cold eve's declining', flatly refuses to merge itself into any sonata movement, and loftily asserts itself in right of ancient descent as entitled to walk before any symphony that ever professor penned.

It is only in the second subject of this movement, an original theme of the composer's own minting, that the form and the material really combine chemically into sonata. And this satisfactory result is presently upset by the digression to the utterly incompatible aim of the composer to display the charms of his native folk-music. In the first movement the sonata writer keeps to his point better: there are no national airs lifted bodily into it. Nevertheless the first movement does not convince me that Professor Stanford's talent is a symphonic talent any more than Meyerbeer's was. In mentioning Meyerbeer I know I run the risk of having the implied comparison interpreted in the light of the Wagnerian criticism – that is, as a deliberate disparagement. I do not mean it so. The Wagnerian criticism of Meyerbeer is valid only as a page in the history of the development of opera into Wagnerian music-drama. Taken out of this connection it will not stand verification for a moment.

If you try to form a critical scheme of the development of English poetry from Pope to Walt Whitman, you cannot by any stretch of ingenuity make a place in it for Thomas Moore, who is accordingly either ignored in such schemes or else contemptuously dismissed as a flowery trifler. In the same way you cannot get Meyerbeer into the Wagnerian scheme except as the Autolycus of the piece. But this proves nothing except that criticism cannot give an absolutely true and just account of any artist: it can at best explain its point of view and then describe the artist from that point of view. You have only to shift yourself an inch to the right or left of my own point of view to find this column full of grotesque exaggerations and distortions; and if you read the musical papers you will sometimes find some *naïf* doing this, and verdantly assuming that *his* point of view commands the absolute truth and that I am the father of lies.

Let me therefore make it clear that I am not likening Stanford to Meyerbeer from the Wagnerian point of view. I am thinking of Meyerbeer's individual characteristics as a composer: for instance, the singularity which is not always originality, the inventiveness which is not always fecundity, the love of the curious and piquant, the fastidious industry and cleverness, the intense and jealous individualism with its resultant treatment of the executants as mere instruments and not as artistic comrades and co-operators, the retreating from any effect that cannot be exactly and mechanically planned by himself as from an impossibility, the love of the fantastic, legendary, non-human element in folk-music (compare Stanford's settings of Irish songs with Dinorah), and the almost selfishly concentrated feeling, the fire, the distinction, the passion that flash out occasionally through much artifice and much trifling.

The parallel is of course not exact; and the temperament indicated by it does not disqualify Stanford from writing symphonies any more than it disqualified Raff; but it suggests my view of the composer of the Irish Symphony as compendiously as is possible within present limits. With the right sort of book, and the right sort of opportunity in other respects, Stanford might produce a powerful and brilliant opera without creating any of the amazement which would certainly be caused by any such feat on the part of his academic rivals.

The performance of the Irish Symphony was decisively successful. Except to briefly and gratefully note a marked improvement on the part of the Philharmonic band, I can say nothing more at present. Dozens of pianists and other concert-givers are hereby begged to excuse me until next week.

Saint-Saëns

→►◄←

7 June 1893

I HAVE to congratulate the Philharmonic Society on having at last made a resolute and fairly successful effort to give a concert of nearly reasonable length. Instead of the usual two or three concertos, five or six symphonies, selection of overtures, suite from the latest 'incidental music' composed for the theatres by one of our professors, and a march or so, besides the vocal pieces, we had only about two hours' music; and though that is a good half-hour too much, still, it is better than two hours and forty or fifty minutes. We also had the orchestra under the command of conductors who, as their own works were in hand, were strongly interested in making the most of the occasion; and the result was instructive.

Saint-Saëns' Rouet d'Omphale is trivial enough to satisfy even the weariest of the unhappy persons who go to the Philharmonic for the sake of culture, under compulsion of fashion or their parents, and who invariably betray themselves by the rapture with which they greet any of those bogus concertos or symphonies which are really only very slightly developed *suites de ballet*, with episcopal barcarolles disguised as 'second subjects'. But it afforded the relief of contemplating a broad expanse of finely graded sound between the *fortissimo* of the band as Saint-Saëns handled it and its *pianissimo*. There were ten degrees of color and force in the gradation where there is usually only one; and even these did not exhaust the possible range of effect, for the orchestra is capable of a much more powerful *fortissimo* than Saint-Saëns required from it.

Again, in the scherzo of Tchaikowsky's symphony, a movement of purely orchestral display, the quality of tone in the *pizzicato* for the strings and in the section for the brass was wonderful. Probably Tchaikowsky could not have achieved such a result anywhere else in the world at equally short notice. But why is it that but for the occasional visits of strangers like Grieg, Tchaikowsky, and Saint-Saëns, we should never know what our best London band can do? Solely, I take it, because the visitors are virtually independent of that impossible body of hardened malversators of our English funds of musical skill, the Philharmonic directors. For their displeasure the distinguished foreign composer does not care a brass farthing: he comes and instals himself at the rehearsals, making their insufficiency suffice for his own work by prolonging and monopolizing them.

On the other hand, the official conductor is the slave of the directors: if he complains to them they take no notice of his complaints: if he complains to the public, as Mr Cowen did in desperation, they dismiss him, knowing, unfortunately, that there will be no difficulty in finding someone else to take his place, which, except artistically, is a highly desirable one.

This season, thanks to the scandal of Mr Cowen's complaint and dismissal, and to such tweaking of the Philharmonic nose, and tripping up of its heels, and unexpected hurling of sharp cornered bricks at its third waistcoat button as those critics who have the Society's interests really at heart can find time for, there has been an improvement, of which I, for one, have given rather exaggerated accounts for the better encouragement of the directors in the right path; but, after all, here I am face to face with a concert in which the band did admirable work under the batons of Russian and French strangers, whilst, under the official conductor, it played the accompaniment to Isolde's Liebestod in a way that would have fully justified poor Miss Macintyre in sending for the police.

To make that song produce no effect whatever may seem hardly feasible; but the Philharmonic band – this very same band that distinguished itself so remarkably in Tchaikowsky's symphony a few minutes later – did it quite easily. I need not describe the familiar process – the parts read off with businesslike insensibility at a steady *mezzo-forte*, and with just enough artistic habit to make the result presentable to those who were unacquainted with the work. That is the sort of thing that turns me from a reasonable and indulgent critic into a mere musical dynamitard. . . .

Brahms

-+->-<+-

21 June 1893

A CONCERT of chamber music selected exclusively from the works of Johannes Brahms is not supposed to be the sort of entertainment to put me into the highest good-humor. Herein, however, I am wronged. Such a reputation as that of Brahms is not to be won without great talent. Unfortunately, music is still so much of a mystery in this country that people get bewildered if they are told that the same man has produced an execrable requiem and an excellent sonata. There seems to them to be no sense in going on in this inconsistent way; for clearly a requiem is a musical composition, and if a man composes it badly he is a bad composer; and a bad composer cannot compose a good sonata, since that also is a musical composition. Yet these very people can often see plainly enough that in pictorial art the same man may be an admirable decorative designer, colorist, or landscape painter, and an atrocious figure draughtsman; or, in literature, that good stories and bad plays, charming poems and fatuous criticisms, may come from the same hand.

The departments of music are not less various than those of the other arts; and Brahms is no more to be disposed of by the condemnation as tedious, commonplace, and incoherent, of those works of his which profess an intellectual or poetic basis than – well, the comparisons which offer themselves are numerous and tempting; but perhaps I had better leave them alone. Suffice it to say that whilst Brahms is successful neither as an intellectual nor a poetic composer, but only as a purely sensuous musician, his musical sense is so much more developed than that of the average audience that many of the harmonies and rhythms which are to him simply voluptuous and impetuous, sound puzzling and imposing to the public, and are therefore surmised to be profoundly intellectual.

To me it seems quite obvious that the real Brahms is nothing more than a sentimental voluptuary with a wonderful ear. For respectability's sake he adopts the forms academically supposed to be proper to great composers, since it gives him no trouble to pile up *points d'orgue*, as in the Requiem, or to call a childishly sensuous reverie on a few simple chords, arranged into the simplest of strains for chaconne purposes by Handel, a set of variations on a theme by that master, or to adapt a ramble in search of fresh delights more or less to sonata form; but you have only to compare his symphonies and quintets with those of Beethoven or Mozart to become conscious that he is the most wanton of composers, that he is only ingenious in his wantonness, and that when his ambition leads him to turn his industry in any other direction his charm does not turn with it, and he becomes the most superficial and irrelevant of formalists.

Only, his wantonness is not vicious: it is that of a great baby, gifted enough to play with harmonies that would baffle most grown-up men, but still a baby, never more happy than when he has a crooning song to play with, always ready for the rocking-horse and the sugar-stick, and rather tiresomely addicted to dressing himself up as Handel or Beethoven and making a prolonged and intolerable noise. That this masquerade of his has taken in a considerable number of persons in Berlin and London is easily explicable on the hypothesis that they see no more in Handel or Beethoven than Brahms can imitate; but again you have only to compare the agonies of lassitude undergone by a Requiem audience with the general purring over his violin concerto, or the encores Miss Lehmann gets for his cradle songs, to see that Monsieur Tout-le-Monde is not in the least taken in, though he does not venture to say so in the teeth of eminent counsel's opinion to the effect that he ought to be. . . .

Concert Agents

→>—<←

12 July 1893

. . . Somehow, Slivinski has not, so far, been very handsomely treated here. When he first appeared he shewed technical powers of an altogether extraordinary kind: his mere displays of execution – in some of Liszt's operatic fantasias, for example – were intensely interesting and brilliant. His style and force were essentially of the order needed for large audiences and large halls; and one felt that the strain of these was essential to his continued development as an artist. He came, too, at a moment when what was wanted above all things, from a business point of view, was a rival to Paderewski. Slivinski, on the whole, might have played that part better than anyone else had he been vigorously seconded. But we have no great captains in the concert industry nowadays: our agents wait, dreaming Alnaschar dreams, until some single mighty artist makes a success, and then content themselves with running that artist for all he has made himself worth. This is very well as far as it goes; but it leaves to the artists and the public the work that should be done by the *entrepreneur* – the work, that is, of making them acquainted with one another. And when the public is very full of an established favorite, and is convinced that when it has heard him play it has heard everything it ought to hear, and may now go home and have done with the classics, any later arrival, however remarkable, cannot get adequately recognized without some determined, skilful, and long-sighted business handling – unless, indeed, he is a supreme genius, and can oust the favorite. Now, a player good enough to oust Sarasate or Joachim, for instance, is not reasonably possible. When a player like Isaÿe comes to London, he finds that Sarasate and Joachim are supposed to represent all the first-rate violin-playing there is in the world; and when he suggests that he too can fiddle a little, he finds only two sorts of agents: the one who says, 'But I have got Sarasate, and I shall be ruined if the British public discovers that there is any other violinist extant'; and the one who sighs, and says, 'Ah, if only I could get hold of Sarasate, what could I not make him!' The net result being, of course, that Isaÿe, unaccustomed to be treated as a second-rater, and tired of agents who throw away the king of trumps because they cannot have the ace, gives up London as a bad job, to our infinite artistic loss. Slivinski has hitherto, it seems to me, been in much the same predicament. The business of making a reputation for him, as far as that is a business matter, has not attracted British enterprise, either because he is not Paderewski, or because he would be a dangerous rival to Paderewski. Of course this may be a sound business policy for anything I know to the contrary; but from the point of view of the interest of the public, which is the one I am bound to take, whether the public understands its interest or not, it is altogether unsatisfactory, since it ends in a little pianoforte-playing by Paderewski at doubled prices, and a great deal by third-rate players at practically no prices at all; whilst artists like Sapellnikoff, Stavenhagen, De Greef, Sophie Menter, and Agatha Backer Gröndhal (to mention only those whose names occur to me hastily) seem, after a trial or two, to prefer every other musical centre in Europe to London. Instead of getting our reasonable annual share of the best European art in all departments, we find the business of organizing the supply monstrously overdone one year, not done at all for the two years following, timidly underdone the fourth year, profusely but cheaply done the next year if the underdoing has proved encouraging, and finally overdone again the following year out of mere business jealousy – with, of course, a recurring cycle of depression following as before. . . .

Gilbert and Sullivan

→+—◄—

11 October 1893

PLEASANT it is to see Mr Gilbert and Sir Arthur Sullivan working together again full brotherly. They should be on the best of terms; for henceforth Sir Arthur can always say, 'Any other librettist would do just as well: look at Haddon Hall'; whilst Mr Gilbert can retort, 'Any other musician would do just as well: look at The Mountebanks.' Thus have the years of divorce cemented the happy reunion at which we all assisted last Saturday. The twain still excite the expectations of the public as much as ever. How Trial by Jury and The Sorcerer surprised the public, and how Pinafore, The Pirates, and Patience kept the sensation fresh, can be guessed by the youngest man from the fact that the announcement of a new Savoy opera always throws the middle-aged playgoer into the attitude of expecting a surprise. As for me, I avoid this attitude, if only because it is a middle-aged one. Still, I expect a good deal that I could not have hoped for when I first made the acquaintance of comic opera.

Those who are old enough to compare the Savoy performances with those of the dark ages, taking into account the pictorial treatment of the fabrics and colors on the stage, the cultivation and intelligence of the choristers, the quality of the orchestra, and the degree of artistic good breeding, so to speak, expected from the principals, best know how great an advance has been made by Mr D'Oyly Carte in organizing and harmonizing that complex co-operation of artists of all kinds which goes to make up a satisfactory operatic performance. Long before the run of a successful Savoy opera is over Sir Arthur's melodies are dinned into our ears by every promenade band and street piano, and Mr Gilbert's sallies are quoted threadbare by conversationalists and journalists; but the whole work as presented to eye and ear on the Savoy stage remains unhackneyed.

Further, no theatre in London is more independent of those executants whose personal popularity enables them to demand ruinous salaries; and this is not the least advantageous of the differences between opera as the work of a combination of manager, poet, and musician, all three making the most of one another in their concerted striving for the common object of a completely successful representation, and opera as the result of a speculator picking up a libretto, getting somebody with a name to set it to music, ordering a few tradesmen to 'mount' it, and then, with a stage manager hired here, an acting manager hired there, and a popular prima donna, comedian, and serpentine dancer stuck in at reckless salaries like almonds into an underdone dumpling, engaging some empty theatre on the chance of the affair 'catching on'.

If any capitalist wants to succeed with comic opera, I can assure him that he can do so with tolerable security if he only possesses the requisite managerial ability. There is no lack of artistic material for him to set to work on: London is overstocked with artistic talent ready to the hand of anyone who can recognize it and select from it. The difficulty is to find the man with this power of recognition and selection. The effect of the finer artistic temperaments and talents on the ordinary speculator is not merely nil (for in that case he might give them an engagement by accident), but antipathetic. People sometimes complain of the indifference of the public and the managers to the highest elements in fine art. There never was a greater mistake. The Philistine is not indifferent to fine art: he *hates* it.

The relevance of these observations will be apparent when I say that, though I enjoyed the score of Utopia more than that of any of the previous Savoy operas, I am quite prepared to hear that it is not as palatable to the majority of the human race — otherwise the mob — as it was to me. It is written with an artistic absorption and enjoyment of which Sir Arthur Sullivan always had moments, but which seem to have become constant with him only since he was knighted, though I do not suggest that the two things stand in the relation of cause and effect. The orchestral work is charmingly humorous; and as I happen to mean by this only what I say, perhaps I had better warn my readers not to infer that Utopia is full of buffooneries with the bassoon and piccolo, or of patter and tum-tum.

Whoever can listen to such caressing wind parts – zephyr parts, in fact – as those in the trio for the King and the two Judges in the first act, without being coaxed to feel pleased and amused, is not fit even for treasons, stratagems, and spoils; whilst anyone whose ears are capable of taking in more than one thing at a time must be tickled by the sudden busyness of the orchestra as the city man takes up the parable. I also confidently recommend those who go into solemn academic raptures over themes 'in diminution' to go and hear how prettily the chorus of the Christy Minstrel song (borrowed from the plantation dance Johnnie, get a gun) is used, very much in diminution, to make an exquisite mock-banjo accompaniment. In these examples we are on the plane, not of the bones and tambourine, but of Mozart's accompaniments to Soave sia il vento in Cosi fan tutte and the entry of the gardener in Le Nozze di Figaro. Of course these things are as much thrown away on people who are not musicians as a copy of Fliegende Blätter on people who do not read German, whereas anyone can understand mere horseplay with the instruments.

But people who are not musicians should not intrude into opera-houses: indeed, it is to me an open question whether they ought to be allowed to exist at all. As to the score generally, I have only one fault to find with Sir Arthur's luxurious ingenuity in finding pretty timbres of all sorts, and that is that it still leads him to abuse the human voice most unmercifully. I will say nothing about the part he has written for the unfortunate soprano, who might as well leave her lower octave at home for all the relief she gets from the use of her upper one. But take the case of Mr Scott Fishe, one of Mr Carte's most promising discoveries, who did so much to make the ill-fated Jane Annie endurable.

What made Mr Fishe's voice so welcome was that it was neither the eternal callow baritone nor the growling bass: it rang like a genuine 'singing bass'; and one felt that here at last was a chance of an English dramatic *basso cantante*, able to 'sing both high and low', and to contrast his high D with an equally fine one an octave below. Unfortunately, the upper fifth of Mr Fishe's voice, being flexible and of excellent quality, gives him easy command (on occasion) of high passages; and Sir Arthur has ruthlessly seized on this to write for him an excessively specialized baritone part, in which we get not one of those deep, ringing tones which relieved the Jane Annie music so attractively. I have in my time heard so many singers reduced by parts of this sort, in the operas of Verdi and Gounod, to a condition in which they could bawl F sharps *ad lib.* at high pressure, but could neither place a note accurately nor produce any tolerable tone from B flat downwards, that I always protest against vocal parts, no matter what voice they are written for, if they do not employ the voice all over its range, though lying mainly where the singer can sing continuously without fatigue.

A composer who uses up young voices by harping on the prettiest notes in them is an ogreish voluptuary; and if Sir Arthur does not wish posterity either to see the stage whitened with the bones of his victims or else to hear his music transposed wholesale, as Lassalle transposes Rigoletto, he should make up his mind whether he means to write for a tenor or a baritone, and place the part accordingly. Considering that since Santley retired from the stage and Jean de Reszke turned tenor all the big reputations have been made by *bassi cantanti* like Édouard de Reszke and Lassalle, and that all the great Wagner parts in which reputations of the same calibre will be made for some time to come are impossible to completely specialized baritones, I venture, as a critic who greatly enjoys Mr Fishe's performance, to recommend him to ask the composer politely not to treat him worse than Mozart treated Don Giovanni, than Wagner treated Wolfram, or than Sir Arthur himself would treat a clarinet. Miss

Nancy McIntosh, who was introduced to us, it will be remembered, by Mr Henschel at the London Symphony Concerts, where she sang in a selection from Die Meistersinger and in the Choral Symphony, came through the trials of a most inconsiderate vocal part very cleverly, evading the worst of the strain by a treatment which, if a little flimsy, was always pretty. She spoke her part admirably, and, by dint of natural tact, managed to make a positive advantage of her stage inexperience, so that she won over the audience in no time. As to Miss Brandram, Mr Barrington (who by means of a remarkable pair of eyebrows transformed himself into a surprising compound of Mr Goschen and the late Sir William Cusins), Messrs Denny, Kenningham, Le Hay, Gridley, and the rest, everybody knows what they can do; and I need only particularize as to Miss Owen and Miss Florence Perry, who gave us some excellent pantomime in the very amusing lecture scene, contrived by Mr Gilbert, and set to perfection by Sir Arthur, in the first act.

The book has Mr Gilbert's lighter qualities without his faults. Its main idea, the Anglicization of Utopia by a people boundlessly credulous as to the superiority of the English race, is as certain of popularity as that reference to England by the Gravedigger in Hamlet, which never yet failed to make the house laugh. There is, happily, no plot; and the stage business is fresh and well invented – for instance, the lecture already alluded to, the adoration of the troopers by the female Utopians, the Cabinet Council 'as held at the Court of St James's Hall', and the quadrille, are capital strokes. As to the 'Drawing Room', with *débutantes*, cards, trains, and presentations all complete, and the little innovation of a cup of tea and a plate of cheap biscuits, I cannot vouch for its verisimilitude, as I have never, strange as it may appear, been present at a Drawing Room; but that is exactly why I enjoyed it, and why the majority of the Savoyards will share my appreciation of it.

The Need for Cutting

+>-<+

25 October 1893

AFTER the Gounod numbers came an orchestral prelude to The
Eumenides of Aeschylus, by Mr W. Wallace, whose Passing of
Beatrice made some mark last year. Like that work, it shewed
that Mr Wallace knows how to use every instrument except the
scissors. It is all that a young man's work ought to be, imaginative, ambitious, impetuous, romantic, prodigal, and most horribly
indiscriminate. Mr Wallace's imagination is so susceptible, and
his critical faculty so unsuspicious, that when he once gets exalted
he will keep pegging away at a figure long after it has been
worn threadbare, or he will remind you, in the thick of The
Eumenides, of the bathers' chorus in Les Huguenots, because he
cannot resist a few rushing bassoon scales. If every bar in the
overture were as good as the best, it would be very good; and if
every bar were as bad as the worst, it would be very bad : further
than that I decline to go, as there is no saying what Mr Wallace
would be at next if he were rashly encouraged. . . .

Berlioz's *Faust* and Cowen's *Water Lily*

+>-<+

8 November 1893

WHEN the fierce strain put by my critical work on my powers of
attention makes it necessary for me to allow my mind to ramble
a little by way of relief, I like to go to the Albert Hall to hear one
of the performances of the Royal Choral Society. I know nothing
more interesting in its way than to wake up occasionally from a
nap in the amphitheatre stalls, or to come out of a train of political or philosophic speculation, to listen for a few moments to an
adaptation of some masterpiece of music to the tastes of what is
called 'the oratorio public'. Berlioz' Faust is a particularly stiff

subject for Albert Hall treatment. To comb that wild composer's hair, stuff him into a frock-coat and tall hat, stick a hymn-book in his hand, and obtain reverent applause for his ribald burlesque of an Amen chorus as if it were a genuine Handelian solemnity, is really a remarkable feat, and one which few conductors except Sir Joseph Barnby could achieve. Instead of the brimstonish orgy in Auerbach's cellar we have a *soirée* of the Young Men's Christian Association; the drunken blackguardism of Brander is replaced by the decorous conviviality of a respectable young bank clerk obliging with a display of his baritone voice (pronounced by the local pianoforte tuner equal to Hayden Coffin's); Faust reminds one of the gentleman in Sullivan's Sweethearts; the whiskered pandoors and the fierce hussars on the banks of the Danube become a Volunteer corps on the banks of the Serpentine; and all Brixton votes Berlioz a great composer, and finds a sulphurous sublimity in the whistles on the piccolo and clashes of the cymbals which bring Mr Henschel, as Mephistopheles, out of his chair. This does not mean that Berlioz has converted Brixton: it means that Brixton has converted Berlioz. Such conversions are always going on. The African heathen 'embrace' the Christian religion by singing a Te Deum instead of dancing a war-dance after 'wetting their spears' in the blood of the tribe next door; the English heathen (a much more numerous body) take to reading the Bible when it is edited for them by Miss Marie Corelli; the masses, sceptical as to Scott and Dumas, are converted to an appreciation of romantic literature by Mr Rider Haggard; Shakespear and Goethe become world-famous on the strength of 'acting versions' that must have set them fairly spinning in their graves; and there is a general appearance of tempering the wind to the shorn lamb, which turns out, on closer examination, to be really effected by building a badly ventilated suburban villa round the silly animal, and telling him that the frowsy warmth he begins to feel is that of the sunbeam playing on Parnassus, or the peace of mind that passeth all understanding, according to circumstances. When I was young, I was like all immature critics : I used to throw stones at the windows of the villa, and thrust in my head and bawl at the lamb that he was a fool, and that the villa builders – honest people enough, according to their lights – were swindlers and hypocrites, and nincompoops and sixth-raters. But the lamb got on better with them than with me; and at last it struck me that he was happier and more civilized in his villa than shivering in the keen Parnassian winds that delighted my hardier bones; so that now I have become quite fond of him, and love to lead him out when the weather is exceptionally mild (the wind being in the Festival cantata quarter perhaps), and talk to him a bit without letting him see too plainly what a deplorable mutton-head he is. Dropping the metaphor, which is becoming unmanageable, let me point out that the title of Berlioz' work is The Damnation of Faust, and that the most natural abbreviation would be, not Berlioz' Faust, but Berlioz' Damnation. Now the Albert Hall audience would certainly not feel easy with such a phrase in their mouths. I have even noticed a certain reluctance on the part of mixed assemblies of ladies and gentlemen unfamiliar with the German language to tolerate discussions of Wagner's Götterdämmerung, unless it were mentioned only as The Dusk of the Gods. Well, the sole criticism I have to make of the Albert Hall performance is that the damnation has been lifted from the work. It has been 'saved', so to speak, and jogs along in a most respectable manner. The march, which suggests household troops cheered by enthusiastic nursemaids, is encored; and so is the dance of sylphs, which squeaks like a tune on the hurdy-gurdy. The students' Jam nox stellata sounds as though middle-aged commercial travellers were having a turn at it. On the whole the performance, though all the materials and forces for a good one are at the conductor's disposal, is dull and suburban. The fact is, Berlioz is not Sir Joseph Barnby's affair. On Thursday last (note that the concert night is changed back again from Wednesday to Thursday) Gounod's Religious March was played, as at the Crystal Palace. A printed slip was circulated asking the audience to stand up. What value a demonstration manufactured in this way can have I do not see, especially when the performance of the march at the Crystal Palace had proved that it would not have occurred spontaneously. It jarred on me as a forced and flunkeyish manoeuvre; and I took no part in it. I have sufficient feeling about Gounod not to permit myself to be instructed in the matter by impertinent persons communicating with me by anonymous slips of paper. Besides, I object to confer on a trumpery *pièce d'occasion* the distinction which is the traditional English appanage of Handel's Hallelujah Chorus.

My great difficulty in describing Mr Cowen's Norwich Festival cantata, The Water Lily, is to find a point of view sufficiently remote from common sense to enable me to keep my countenance during the process. The most ordinary decencies of professional etiquette bind me to accept with enthusiasm the lines of my distinguished fellow-critic. For instance:

> Though I know not where thou art,
> Well I know thou hast my heart.

> . . . .

> Nor so long be coyly hiding,
> In my arms is thy abiding.

> . . . .

> He is thine, and oer the tide
> Thou shalt go to be his bride,
> Yield thee to love's soft allure,
> Never lived a knight so pure.

If I am ever paid to write a libretto in this style, I will simply buy a bushel of Christmas-cards and fall to with scissors and paste. But then I have not the true poetic gift. The worst of it is that Mr Cowen evidently has not got it either; for he has found no inspiration in Mr Bennett's numbers. Perhaps he did not want it: it may be that as long as Mr Cowen has any sort of *locus standi* for his orchestrating and modulating he is happy. But in that case I beg to say emphatically that I am not. The English horn is a very pretty instrument; and when it has some real work to do, as in the third act of Tristan, I am delighted to hear it. But when, having nothing to do, it insists on shewing itself off to me instead of holding its tongue, I find it an impertinent bore. Similarly, that pet transition from one major common chord to another lying a semitone higher, is magical in the first scene of the third act of Siegfried, where it has some very momentous business to transact; but a mere row of samples of it does not seem to me a fair equivalent for a piece of original composition.

Mr Cowen is too old now to be allowed to play with chords as children do with scraps of colored paper, or even as Mozart and Rossini, in their nonage, played with the ordinary dominant cadence. Some of Mr Cowen's little harmonic sweetmeats are by no means to my taste. It seems a hopelessly obsolete thing to quarrel with a composer for 'false relations' nowadays; but still there is reason in everything. Take the case of a phrase in the key of A flat major stepping off C to B flat in order to spring up immediately to E flat, and accompanied in simple two-part harmony by A flat, G, C. Is it good sense, or rather good sound, to make the G flat, unless you want to shew that the old prohibition of false relations and consecutive major intervals had something in it after all?

What matter if the G natural would make the phrase remind everyone of the love-duet in Gounod's Faust? Better that than the suggestion of a wrong note. However, I suppose Mr Cowen likes it. I can only repeat doggedly, bigotedly, irreconcilably, that I dont. Why should I? If it were expressive of the accompanying words I should accept it without question – without consciousness, probably. But it is set to the words 'Sleep and dream.' Who on earth dreams of 'false relations'? ...

Young Violinists and Goetz

22 November 1893

I CONTINUE to be amazed at the way in which the younger generation plays the fiddle. Formerly there were only two sorts of violinists: the Paganinis or Sivoris, and the bad amateurs whose highest flight was an execrable attempt to scrape through a variation or two on The Carnival of Venice. The orchestral players I leave out altogether; for the trade knack they picked up under stress of bread-winning had nothing to do with violin-playing, as one found out when they got promoted to the leader's desk, and had to play an obbligato occasionally. Nowadays all that is changed in the most bewildering manner. Europe appears to be full of young ladies between twenty and thirty who can play all the regulation concertos – Beethoven, Mendelssohn, Brahms, Bruch, and Saint-Saëns – and throw in Bach's chaconne in D minor as a solo piece at the end of the concert.

And yet they are not geniuses, though they do with apparent ease the things that only geniuses used to do. I should be tempted to put it all down to the terrific determination with which women are qualifying themselves in all branches for an independent career, were it not that the improvement is discoverable in the young men also – though, of course, no male can hope for such chances of shewing his mettle as are offered readily enough to young women. The fact is, people do not like concertos for their own sake. A concerto must have a hero or a heroine; and every plucky and passably pretty feminine violinist under thirty is a heroine in the imagination of the male audience; whereas a callow young man is not anybody's hero, having no touch of that art of personal beauty and dignity at which every woman with grit enough to face the public at all is at least a passable amateur. He can only play the hero if he is a real genius, whereas his female rival will be heroine enough for the public if she has worked hard enough to be able to play the concerto as her master tells her to play it. Hence we have half a dozen young ladies getting first-rate chances every season, whilst young men who can play as well, or better, languish for years unheard.

Take the case of Mr August Manns, for instance. His generosity to young gentlemen with unperformed orchestral scores is the theme of all our praises at present; and he is a second father to Miss Mary Cardew, Miss Frida Scotta, Miss Beatrice Langley, and the rest of our young lady violinists. But may I suggest to him that as all young gentlemen compose very much alike, and all young ladies play very much alike, it would be a relief if he were to transpose the sexes next season, and treat us to a series of compositions by young women and violin concerto performances by young men.

The fact is, I am getting tired of ladylike versions of Bruch's concerto in G minor – very agreeable and skilful, certainly, but utterly unmemorable. I was greatly pleased with Miss Beatrice Langley's playing of it at the Crystal Palace the other day: her youth, her dexterity, and her quick and delicate musical feeling would have earned her a handsome tribute of praise and encouragement from me a few years ago; but today, somehow, my mind keeps going back to that note at the end of the program: 'This concerto was last played at the Saturday Concerts on February 25th, 1893, by Miss Mary Cardew.' I was at that concert; and I remember being 'greatly pleased' by Miss Mary Cardew's performance – quite astonished, in fact, by her execution of the Bach chaconne.

But I had completely forgotten the concerto when the paragraph re-informed – not reminded – me of it. That may be my own fault, or Max Bruch's; and yet I do not forget Isaÿe's performances of Bruch. Anyhow, I plead for a chance for the young male fiddler. However unattractive his sex may be, it must at least produce some small percentage of the beginners who deserve a chance with a concerto at our leading orchestral concerts.

The concert at which Miss Langley made her success, and, let me add, shewed some spirit and common sense by giving the eternal Saint-Saëns a rest, and introducing a welcome novelty in the shape of a capriccio for violin and orchestra by Niels Gade, also gave a lift to Mr Granville Bantock, whose Caedmar, produced by Signor Lago, made us all curious about his overture, The Fire Worshippers. Unluckily, The Fire Worshippers turned out to be an earlier work than Caedmar, mainly occupied with a six-eight movement which was as pure Mendelssohn as Caedmar was pure Wagner. It explained why Mr Bantock got the Macfarren Scholarship at the R.A.M.; but it threw no new light on his development. The Mendelssohn Worshippers was followed by a performance of the Lohengrin prelude in A, finely executed by the wind, and very poorly indeed by the strings. The gem of the concert was Goetz' symphony, which has fallen into neglect because, I suppose, it is the only real symphony that has been composed since Beethoven died. Beside it Mendelssohn's Scotch symphony is no symphony at all, but only an enchanting *suite de pièces*; Schubert's symphonies seem mere debauches of exquisitely musical thoughtlessness; and Schumann's, though genuinely symphonic in ambition, fall short in actual composition. Goetz alone among the modern symphonists is easily and unaffectedly successful from beginning to end.

He has the charm of Schubert without his brainlessness, the refinement and inspiration of Mendelssohn without his limitation and timid gentility, Schumann's sense of harmonic expression without his laboriousness, shortcoming, and dependence on external poetic stimulus; while as to unembarrassed mastery of the material of music, shewing itself in the Mozartian grace and responsiveness of his polyphony, he leaves all three of them simply nowhere. Brahms, who alone touches him in mere brute musical faculty, is a dolt in comparison to him.

You have to go to Mozart's finest quartets and quintets on the one hand, and to Die Meistersinger on the other, for work of the quality we find, not here and there, but continuously, in the symphony in F and in The Taming of the Shrew, two masterpieces which place Goetz securely above all other German composers of the last hundred years, save only Mozart and Beethoven, Weber and Wagner. Of course, if Goetz were alive this would be an excellent reason for opposing him tooth and nail, for the same reasons that moved Salieri to oppose Mozart. A very little Goetz would certainly spoil the market for Festival symphonies; but now that the man is dead, why may we not have the symphony made a stock-piece at the London Symphony and Richter concerts, and performed oftener than once in four years at the Crystal Palace?

There is that beautiful Spring Overture, too, which the lamented Macfarren denounced as containing unlawful consecutive sevenths. Are we never to hear those consecutive sevenths again? Is it to be always Brahms and Bruch and Liszt, until our rising generation loses all sense of the subtle but immense difference between first-rate and second-rate in contemporary symphonic music? ...

Genoveva

→>→←←

13 December 1893

THE chief musical event of last week was the performance of Schumann's Genoveva for the first time on the English stage by the students of the Royal College of Music. The pit and galleries of Drury Lane (handsomely lent for the occasion) were crammed with students. Parents and uncles and aunts of students were everywhere, interrupting the performance in the wrongest possible places by untimely applause, and feeling that such incomprehensible and solemn music as Schumann's must be excellent training for young people. The stalls and boxes were full of critics and other distinguished persons. Speaking as one of them, may I suggest that when we are so numerous, and consequently so tightly packed, the management should have a steam crane on the site of the prompter's box between the acts, so that any critic desiring to leave his place during the intervals could hook himself by the waistband to the end of the chain and be hoisted out of his seat, swung round, and dropped at the door nearest the refreshment bar?

The orchestra, being nearly eighty strong, was responsible for some of the packing. It was quite the most brilliant part of the house, as thirty-four out of fifty of the strings were young women, most of them so attractive that for once the average of personal beauty was higher in the band than on the stage. The swarming and chattering when they assembled, and the irreverent waving of bows to friends in the house, put everybody into good humor – even those critics who were furious at having to begin their afternoon's work as early as half past one.

Genoveva was an excellent selection for the College to make. Since it is commercially valueless as an opera, we should never have heard it at all if it had not been taken in hand by a purely academic institution; and yet, being by Schumann, it was certain that some interesting music lay buried in it. For Schumann had at least one gift which we have now come to rank very highly among the qualifications of a composer for the stage: to wit, a strong feeling for harmony as a means of emotional expression. There are passages in Genoveva which are in this respect genuinely Wagnerian – and I am not one of those incorrigible people who cry out Wagner whenever they hear an unprepared major 'tonic discord'.

Unfortunately, in the other qualifications of the music-dramatist, Schumann is as far behind Beethoven as Beethoven was behind Mozart and Wagner. To begin with, he gives away all pretension to seriousness in his enterprise by providing as its subject a book which is nakedly silly. He may have persuaded himself – such a folly would have been just like him – that he could make his heroine do for his opera what Beethoven made Leonora do for Fidelio. But Fidelio, though commonplace and homely, is not silly. Its few harmless stage conventions do not prevent it from being credible and human from beginning to end; whereas Genoveva, from the moment when the witch enters in the first act, degenerates into pure bosh, and remains mostly at that level to the end. The witch's music is frivolous and serio-comic, the orchestration sprouting at the top into an outrageous piccolo part which would hardly be let off with mere indulgent laughter if it came from any less well-beloved composer.

In one place, the villain being left with the heroine, who has fainted, he exclaims: 'We are alone.' Immediately – the witch being round the corner – the piccolo utters a prolonged and derisive squawk, as if a cockatoo were reminding him that it had its eye on him. Instrumentation, as we all know, was not Schumann's strong point; and there is plenty of his characteristic orchestral muddling in Genoveva; but I can remember no other instance of his scoring being foolish in its intention. The witch is perhaps not much worse in the early scenes than Sir Arthur Sullivan's Ulrica in Ivanhoe, or in the incantation scene than Verdi's Ulrica in Un Ballo; but one has only to think of Ortrud in Lohengrin to realize the distance that separates Schumann's second-hand ideas from those of a really creative genius.

Another of the failures of Genoveva is Golo, the villain. As he is, unfortunately, a sentimental villain, it would require a Mozartian subtlety of characterization to differentiate him from the other sentimental people in the opera – the hero and heroine, for instance. This subtlety Schumann did not possess: accordingly, Siegfried or Genoveva might sing every bar of Golo's music without the smallest incongruity. Imagine the effect of Don Giovanni singing Leporello's music, Elvira Zerlina's, Wotan Loki's, or Alberich Mime's!

Even Beethoven, whose powers in this respect were so blunt that, like a veritable Procrustes, he levelled four different characters in his Fidelio by writing a quartet in canon for them (conceive Non ti fidar or Un di si ben in canon!), not to mention that his prison porter and gaoler's daughter are absolutely indistinguishable in kind from his Florestan and Leonora – even Beethoven made Pizarro an unmistakeable scoundrel. He could not, like Wagner or Mozart, have given us half a dozen scoundrels, each as distinct from the other as Tartuffe from Harpagon or Rogue Riderhood from Silas Wegg; but he could at least distinguish an amiable person from an unamiable one. But this moderate feat has baffled Schumann in Genoveva.

It is obvious, then, that we must fall back on the symphonic, descriptive, and lyrical pages of the score for such merits as it possesses. In none of these can anything be found that need be heard by anyone who knows Schumann's songs, pianoforte pieces, and symphonies. In the nonsensical magic mirror and ghost scenes of the third act, and the demented business in the ravine in the fourth, Schumann, for the most part, leaves the stage to get on as best it can, and retires into pure symphony, with an effect which is only tolerable on condition of dismissing as so much superfluous rubbish all of the actual drama shewn on the boards, except, perhaps, what may be barely necessary to motivate in the vaguest manner the emotions of Genoveva and her husband.

The opera is at its best when Genoveva is on the stage; and it is never absolutely vulgar and trivial except in the witch music. The departure of the troops in the first act is an effective piece of composition for the stage; and there are one or two episodes in the second act, when Genoveva is alone in her chamber, which are by no means unsuccessful. But the work, as a whole, is a failure; and glad as I am that I have heard it, I cannot blame the world for dropping its acquaintance, though it has left a good many less worthy names on its operatic visiting list.

The performance, conducted by Professor Stanford, went without a hitch. It had been faithfully and thoroughly rehearsed; and the performers, unpaid, and unspoiled by popularity or practical experience of the credulity of that harmless monster, the public, did their very best anxiously and eagerly, the result being, in spite of a hundred comical little accidents due to the nervousness and ineptitude of the performers, a certain satisfactoriness and even a degree of illusion which is the rarest thing in the world at regular professional performances.

The most obtrusively academic part of the affair was the posing, walking, and gesticulation. The unhappy students had been taught 'plastique' until they dared not call their arms and legs their own. The plastique professor, with his principles of beauty, and his set of regulations for the attainment of absolute grace of attitude, is almost as fatal a person as the harmony professor with *his* set of regulations for the attainment of 'correct' part writing. No attitude, unfortunately for professordom, is unconditionally beautiful. Apollo, eight heads high, and with his shoulders broader than his waist, may look like a god in an attitude in which Smith, seven heads high, and with his waist perhaps broader than his champagne-bottle shoulders, may look absurd.

It is all very well to compile principles of beauty from Greek statuary; but the sculptor can shape his man to suit his attitude, whereas the actor has to make the attitude suit the real human shape, which varies so infinitely from one person to another that methods of identifying criminals by their physical proportions are said to be infallible. As an alteration of an inch in the relation between the size of the body and legs or head may make all the difference in the world in the grace of a pose, it is not to be wondered at that people who copy the attitudes and gestures of others – especially of those famous for their grace – at once make themselves ridiculous. There are, in fact, no standard attitudes; and the utmost a teacher can do is to rouse the pupil's conscience on the subject of personal grace, and leave him, under the guidance of that conscience, to grow his own plastique.

This, of course, is not the view taken at the Royal College. The characters in Genoveva were always defying common sense, and even the law of gravitation, in standard attitudes. Golo, in particular, was most conscientious: his profile when he placed his right foot on the castle steps in the first act would have delighted Mr Wopsle's dresser. Later on, however, his efforts to fulfil the precept 'Stand always on one leg' wore him out; and he repeatedly supported himself, in mere exhaustion, on two, very unclassically. Genoveva repulsing him with her right arm stretched out and the hand prettily pronated was also an elegant spectacle. But the attitudes, on the whole, lacked conviction.

The one or two which came off successfully were abstractly beautiful, perhaps; but they would have been the same in any other drama or with any other individuals. I confidently recommend the youthful posers of the College, whilst cultivating strength, grace, and a fine bodily tone to their heart's content, to carefully forget all the attitudes and rules they have been taught. A graceful attitude is an attitude taken spontaneously by a graceful person; and nothing is more hopeless than to attempt to begin with the attitude and work backwards to the person.

The singing was decidedly better than might have been expected. There was no great success like that of Miss Clara Butt last year in Orfeo, though the audience made a sort of attempt to manufacture one by making a heroine of the witch, who was clever, spirited, fluent, and ready, but whose voice and style were rather shallow. Mr Archdeacon (Siegfried) and Miss Bruckshaw (Genoveva) are to be heartily congratulated on the condition in which they have come out of the destructive process of being taught to sing. We shall certainly hear more of Mr Archdeacon, who has an agreeable baritone voice.

Mr Charles Green, unmercifully victimized by academic principles, both in singing and attitudinizing, did his best as Golo. His voice is stronger than it was; but he is still hampered by the bleating method with which he began. If he will earnestly set himself during the forthcoming year to do exactly the reverse of everything he is told, the favorable results of the new departure can be judged in next year's performance. . . .

Noufflard on Wagner

→►◄◄

17 January 1894

IT is not often that one comes across a reasonable book about music, much less an entertaining one. Still, I confess to having held out with satisfaction to the end of M. Georges Noufflard's Richard Wagner d'après lui-même (Paris, Fischbacher, 2 vols., at 3.50 fr. apiece). Noufflard is so exceedingly French a Frenchman that he writes a preface to explain that though he admires Wagner, still Alsace and Lorraine must be given back; and when he records an experiment of his hero's in teetotalism, he naïvely adds, 'What is still more surprising is that this unnatural régime, instead of making Wagner ill, operated exactly as he had expected.' More Parisian than this an author can hardly be; and yet Noufflard always understands the Prussian composer's position, and generally agrees with him, though, being racially out of sympathy with him, he never entirely comprehends him. He is remarkably free from the stock vulgarities of French operatic culture: for instance, he washes his hands of Meyerbeer most fastidiously; and he puts Gluck, the hero of French musical classicism, most accurately in his true place.

And here let me give a piece of advice to readers of books about Wagner. Whenever you come to a statement that Wagner was an operatic reformer, and that in this capacity he was merely following in the footsteps of Gluck, who had anticipated some of his most important proposals, you may put your book in the waste-paper basket, as far as Wagner is concerned, with absolute confidence. Gluck was an opera composer, who said to his contemporaries: 'Gentlemen, let us compose our operas more rationally. An opera is not a stage concert, as most of you seem to think. Let us give up our habit of sacrificing our common sense to the vanity of our singers, and let us compose and orchestrate our airs, our duets, our recitatives, and our sinfonias in such a way that they shall always be appropriate to the dramatic situation given to us by the librettist.' And having given this excellent advice, he proceeded to shew how it could be followed. How well he did this we can judge, in spite of our scandalous ignorance of Gluck, from Orfeo, with which Giulia Ravogli has made us familiar lately.

When Wagner came on the scene, exactly a hundred years later, he found that the reform movement begun by Gluck had been carried to the utmost limits of possibility by Spontini, who told him flatly that after La Vestale, etc., there was nothing operatic left to be done. Wagner quite agreed with him, and never had the smallest intention of beginning the reform of opera over again at the very moment when it had just been finished. On the contrary, he took the fully reformed opera, with all its improvements, and asked the nineteenth century to look calmly at it and say whether all this patchwork of stage effects on a purely musical form had really done anything for it but expose the absurd unreality of its pretence to be a form of drama, and whether, in fact, Rossini had not shewn sound common sense in virtually throwing over that pretence and, like Gluck's Italian contemporaries, treating an opera as a stage concert. The nineteenth century took a long time to make up its mind on the question, which it was at first perfectly incapable of understanding. Verdi and Gounod kept on trying to get beyond Spontini on operatic lines, without the least success, except on the purely musical side; and Gounod never gave up the attempt, though Verdi did.

Meanwhile, however, Wagner, to shew what he meant, abandoned operatic composition altogether, and took to writing dramatic poems, and using all the resources of orchestral harmony and vocal tone to give them the utmost reality and intensity of expression, thereby producing the new art form which he called 'music-drama', which is no more 'reformed opera' than a cathedral is a reformed stone quarry. The whole secret of the amazing futility of the first attempts at Wagner criticism is the mistaking of this new form for an improved pattern of the old one. Once you conceive Wagner as the patentee of certain novel features in operas and librettos, you can demolish him point by point with impeccable logic, and without the least misgiving that you are publicly making a ludicrous exhibition of yourself.

The process is fatally easy, and consists mainly in shewing that the pretended novelties of reformed opera are no novelties at all. The 'leading motives', regarded as operatic melodies recurring in connection with the entry of a certain character, are as old as opera itself; the instrumentation, regarded merely as instrumentation, is no better than Mozart's and much more expensive; whereas of those features that really tax the invention of the operatic composer, the airs, the duos, the quartets, the cabalettas to display the virtuosity of the trained Italian singer, the dances, the marches, the choruses, and so on, there is a deadly dearth, their place being taken by – of all things – an interminable dull recitative.

The plain conclusion follows that Wagner was a barren rascal whose whole reputation rested on a shop-ballad, O star of eve, and a march which he accidentally squeezed out when composing his interminable Tannhäuser. And so you go on, wading with fatuous self-satisfaction deeper and deeper into a morass of elaborately reasoned and highly conscientious error. You need fear nothing of this sort from Noufflard. He knows perfectly well the difference between music-drama and opera; and the result is that he not only does not tumble into blind hero-worship of Wagner, but is able to criticize him – a thing that blunderers never could do. Some of his criticisms: for example, his observation that in Wagner's earlier work the melody is by no means so original as Weber's, are indisputable – indeed he might have said Meyerbeer or anybody else; for Wagner's melody was never original at all in that sense, any more than Giotto's figures are picturesque or Shakespear's lines elegant.

But I entirely – though quite respectfully – dissent from Noufflard's suggestion that in composing Tristan Wagner turned his back on the theoretic basis of Siegfried, and returned to 'absolute music'. It is true, as Noufflard points out, that in Tristan, and even in Der Ring itself, Wagner sometimes got so rapt from the objective drama that he got away from the words too, and in Tristan came to writing music without coherent words at all. But wordless music is not absolute music. Absolute music is the purely decorative sound pattern : tone poetry is the musical expression of poetic feeling. When Tristan gives musical expression to an excess of feeling for which he can find no coherent words, he is no more uttering absolute music than the shepherd who carries on the drama at one of its most deeply felt passages by playing on his pipe.

Wagner regarded all Beethoven's important instrumental works as tone poems; and he himself, though he wrote so much for the orchestra alone in the course of his music-dramas, never wrote, or could write, a note of absolute music. The fact is, there is a great deal of feeling, highly poetic and highly dramatic, which cannot be expressed by mere words – because words are the counters of thinking, not of feeling – but which can be supremely expressed by music. The poet tries to make words serve his purpose by arranging them musically, but is hampered by the certainty of becoming absurd if he does not make his musically arranged words mean something to the intellect as well as to the feeling.

For example, the unfortunate Shakespear could not make Juliet say :

> O Romeo, Romeo, Romeo, Romeo, Romeo;

and so on for twenty lines. He had to make her, in an extremity of unnaturalness, begin to argue the case in a sort of amatory legal fashion, thus :

> O Romeo, Romeo, wherefore art thou Romeo?
> Deny thy father and refuse thy name,
> Or, if thou wilt not, etc., etc., etc.

It is verbally decorative; but it is not love. And again :

> Parting is such sweet sorrow
> That I shall say goodnight till it be morrow;

which is a most ingenious conceit, but one which a woman would no more utter at such a moment than she would prove the rope ladder to be the shortest way out because any two sides of a triangle are together greater than the third.

Now these difficulties do not exist for the tone poet. He can make Isolde say nothing but 'Tristan, Tristan, Tristan, Tristan, Tristan', and Tristan nothing but 'Isolde, Isolde, Isolde, Isolde, Isolde', to their hearts' content without creating the smallest demand for more definite explanations; and as for the number of times a tenor and soprano can repeat 'Addio, addio, addio', there is no limit to it. There is a great deal of this reduction of speech to mere ejaculation in Wagner; and it is a reduction directly pointed to in those very pages of Opera and Drama which seem to make the words all-important by putting the poem in the first place as the seed of the whole music-drama, and yet make a clean sweep of nine-tenths of the dictionary by insisting that it is only the language of feeling that craves for musical expression, or even is susceptible of it.

Nay, you may not only reduce the words to pure ejaculation, you may substitute mere roulade vocalization, or even balder-dash, for them, provided the music sustains the feeling which is the real subject of the drama, as has been proved by many pages of genuinely dramatic music, both in opera and elsewhere, which either have no words at all, or else belie them. It is only when a thought interpenetrated with intense feeling has to be expressed, as in the Ode of Joy in the Ninth Symphony, that coherent words must come with the music. You have such words in Tristan; you have also ejaculations void of thought, though full of feeling; and you have plenty of instrumental music with no words at all. But you have no 'absolute' music, and no 'opera'.

Nothing in the world convinces you more of the fact that a dramatic poem cannot possibly take the form of an opera libretto than listening to Tristan and comparing it with, say, Gounod's Romeo and Juliet. I submit, then, to Noufflard (whose two volumes I none the less cordially recommend to all amateurs who can appreciate a thinker) that the contradictions into which

Wagner has fallen in this matter are merely such verbal ones as are inevitable from the imperfection of language as an instrument for conveying ideas; and that the progress from Der fliegende Holländer to Parsifal takes a perfectly straight line ahead in theory as well as in artistic execution. . . .

Beethoven's Quartets

+>-<+

21 February 1894

. . . I HAVE my own moments of impatience over Beethoven; and an excellent way to produce them is to send me to a Popular Concert without any dinner, and treat me to a Rasoumowsky quartet led by Joachim on the first night of his season here, when, bothered by the change of diapason from Germany to England, and finding that his violin is dragging at the pitch somehow, he begins to worry the movement with a notion that perhaps it will come right if it is only driven hard enough. A tendency to drive is an old fault of Joachim as a quartet leader, though of late years he has so far got over it that when he is quite calm and reconciled to the high pitch, his fine tone and sleeplessly thoughtful style (if we could only get it combined with Sarasate's sleeplessly sensitive and steady hand, what a violinist we should have!) are better worth hearing than ever. But when anything flurries him, you find the critics next day full of that dismally deep respect which bewrays the man who has not liked something he thinks he ought to like.

As for me, I said with my usual irreverence, 'Joachim is flat; and the quartet is not going to be good: I will go and recapture the missing dinner: next week probably he will play splendidly.' The next chamber-music concert I was at, however, was not a Monday Popular, but one given by Mr Gompertz, who unearthed a very good quartet in A minor, by Professor Villiers Stanford, which for some reason had not been performed in public before in London. It is a genuine piece of absolute music, alive with feeling from beginning to end, and free from those Stanfordian aberrations into pure cleverness which remind one so of Brahms' aberrations into pure stupidity.

It is true that the composer has done one or two things for no other reason that I can discover except that Beethoven did something like them; but a professor is bound, I suppose, to shew himself a man of taste; and at all events the passages in question have borrowed some of the fire, as well as the form, of the master. Unfortunately, the quartet is very difficult; and I cannot honestly say that Messrs Gompertz, Inwards, Kreuz, and Ould were quite equal to it. The performance lacked delicacy and precision. Mr Gompertz is a courageous player who affects a certain rough warmth and vigor of style which occasionally finds its opportunity; but he is not fastidious, and Professor Stanford is; so the quartet was not made the most of.

The great attraction for me at this concert was Beethoven's posthumous quartet in C sharp minor. Why should I be asked to listen to the intentional intellectualities, profundities, theatrical fits and starts, and wayward caprices of self-conscious genius which make up those features of the middle period Beethovenism for which we all have to speak so very seriously, when I much prefer these beautiful, simple, straightforward, unpretentious, perfectly intelligible posthumous quartets? Are they to be always avoided because the professors once pronounced them obscure and impossible? Surely the disapproval of these infatuated persons must by this time prejudice all intelligent persons in favor of the works objected to.

The performance, though the opening *adagio* was taken at a tolerably active *andante*, was an enjoyable one – another proof, by the way, that the difficulties of these later works of Beethoven are superstitiously exaggerated. As a matter of fact, they fail much seldomer in performance nowadays than the works of his middle age. . . .

Instruments and Pitch

7 March 1894

MR SCHULZ-CURTIUS announces that the orchestra at the Mottl Wagner Concert at Queen's Hall on April 17 will tune to French pitch. So much the better. I am a confirmed sceptic as to the reality of those poetic differences which musicians imagine they find between one key and another; for I have never known two persons agree as to the alleged characteristics of the keys. Besides, scientific men have explained the differences, and have thereby confirmed my opinion that they do not exist. Accordingly, I do not believe that when the change from Continental to English pitch virtually transposes Beethoven's C minor Symphony into something nearer to C sharp minor, the character and feeling of the composition are totally altered. But neither do I believe anything so foolish as that the difference in absolute pitch does not matter. The difference between the effect of Pop Goes the Weasel played on an oboe and played on a double bassoon is only a matter of absolute pitch; but nobody will deny the difference in the effect on the listener's spirits. And if you take the Funeral March from Götterdämmerung, and play it half a tone higher, you also play it half a tone merrier. Hence the importance of the change announced by Mr Schulz-Curtius.

Another piece of artistic conscientiousness on his part is his promise to provide the four tenor tubas and the bass trumpet for the Nibelungen music. Doubtless the bass trumpet will be a great joy to us; but oh, if we could only get some decent instrument to play the ordinary trumpet parts on! I declare, in all sincerity, to Messrs Ellis, Morrow, and Jaeger that all their skill leaves the cornet as objectionable as ever. I know very well that the slide trumpet of the text-books is an impracticable nuisance; but cannot something be done with more modern inventions? Has not a gentleman – a Mr Wyatt, if I recollect aright – invented a practicable slide trumpet by making the slide a double one and so halving the length of the shifts?

And what about those so-called Bach trumpets and Handel trumpets that Kosleck, of Berlin, introduced to us here at the Bach bi-centenary, and that Mr Morrow occasionally plays? Or, if all these are impossible, are there not at least compensating pistons to correct those notes which come so diabolically out of tune with the ordinary three valves? Instrument-makers like Besson, for instance, solemnly invite the critics and Lord Chelmsford and a few amateurs from time to time to hear such improvements. They seem satisfactory, but are never heard of again. It is just like the experiments which used to take place on the Thames Embankment, when an inventor would build a wooden house, soak it in petroleum, sit down on a heap of shavings in the parlor, set fire to the house, and be found after the conflagration perfectly comfortable and unsinged, thanks to his patent extinguisher or fireproof overcoat, applicable to every household. And yet people go on getting burnt as if such patents had never been heard of.

The fact is, we want some genuine artist to take up the work of producing fine instruments, just as Mr William Morris has taken up the work of producing beautiful printed books. The instrument-makers will never do it, because all their efforts are aimed at better intonation, greater facility of execution, and perfect smoothness of tone. Now smoothness of tone is all very well in its way; but the question remains, what sort of tone? The instrument-makers care only for that one variety, dear to Kneller Hall, which is the true characteristic tone of the saxhorn or euphonium, but which robs the trumpet, the trombone, and the horn of their individuality.

I verily believe that the instrument-makers would like nothing better than to make all the brass in the orchestra sound as if it consisted of a happy family of saxhorns, from the bombardon to the cornet. Their ideal orchestra would consist of the string quartet with a cavalry band for the brass, and a set of English concertinas, bass, tenor, alto, and treble, for the wood wind. That is why I want an artist-craftsman to take the matter up, with the object, not of inventing some new instrument like the saxophone or sarrusophone which nobody wants, but of giving us back the old instruments which everybody wants, with their individuality developed to the utmost.

In short, we want a maker of instruments for the classical orchestra; and we shall certainly not get him on strictly commercial lines at present, because the great bulk of the instrument business lies with military bands, and with the innumerable bands on the military model which exist throughout the country, from those of the Salvation Army to the amateur bands of the industrial counties, which compete as eagerly for prizes as rival football teams do, and which spend considerable sums out of those prizes in perfecting their instrumental equipment.

The extent to which the evolution of the mechanism of the orchestra is altering its artistic character was impressed on me at a recent Crystal Palace Concert, where we had a flute concerto played by Mr Albert Fransella, an excellent artist who has only recently joined Mr Mann's band. Like Sivori the violinist, who died only the other day, and who, by the way, greatly astonished my small boyhood – he was the first virtuoso I ever heard – Mr Fransella sacrifices boldness of style to delicacy of tone and perfection of execution. He takes his instrument as it is, and does not enlarge the holes to get a big tone, or otherwise spoil it for all ordinary players, and trust to his power of lip to make it practicable for himself. What we got from him therefore was the normal modern orchestral flute, very well played.

But I should like to have met the ghost of Mozart at that concert in order to ask him whether Mr Fransella's instrument was what he would call a flute. I am convinced that he would have declared it a quite new instrument. He would, no doubt, have been delighted with the accurate intonation and the fascinating peculiarity and beauty of the lower octave; but I think he would have repudiated the higher notes as having absolutely no flute quality at all, the quality aimed at by the manufacturer being apparently that of the harmonica, though really, no doubt, that of the clarionet. These harmonica-like sounds got on my nerves after a while; and I am not at all sure that I should not have enjoyed Mr Fransella's skill and taste more if he had played a fantasia by Kuhlau or some other eighteenth-century master on an old-fashioned flute. And yet I was so far from being in an old-fashioned humor at this concert that I went home halfway through Schubert's charming symphony in C in a fit of exasperation at its childishness.

Mind, I do not object to the existence and use of these practically new instruments; but I wish they had not usurped the old names; and I still call for the artist-craftsman to give us once more a flute that is a flute, and a trumpet that is a trumpet. When he has done that he may adapt the inventions of Gordon, Sax, and the rest to his masterpieces as much as he pleases; for naturally I do not want the old defects back – the primitive mechanism and the faulty, weak, or missing notes. The intonation of the wind is quite bad enough still, without our turning back to the methods of the old days when it was worse.

Talking of instruments reminds me that the Philharmonic band has only fourteen first and twelve second violins. It ought to have had fifteen of both twenty years ago; and today it ought to employ a hundred men for a fully scored modern work. I did not raise this question while the Society remained in St James's Hall; for one cannot make demands for fresh expenditure without some reference to the size of the hall and the prices charged.

But now that a move has been made to the comparatively huge Queen's Hall, there is no further reason for tolerating a short-handedness that makes a really effective performance of the works of Berlioz and Liszt impossible. Some of the scores on which Berlioz wrote the words 'at least fifteen' before the two violin parts are half a century old now; so it will be seen that I am not unduly hurrying up the venerable directors. They will, I hope, not permit themselves to be beaten in artistic conscientiousness by Mr Schulz-Curtius. And yet I suppose they will disappoint me, as usual. I have no opinion of the Philharmonic directors from the artistic point of view, and never had. Only I think it hard that Art should not have its share of the profit of their move to a larger hall. . . .

Mottl and Wagner

25 April 1894

I MUST entirely applaud Mr Henschel's spirited cutting-in between Herr Felix Mottl and the expectant public with a Wagner program identical, save as to one item (the Flying Dutchman overture), with that announced for Herr Mottl's first appearance in England. I have heard people say that such a challenge was in bad taste; but in this case, as in ninety-nine out of a hundred others in which the same complaint is made, good taste would have meant simply moral cowardice, a quality in which we in England are always anxious to be kept in countenance. Mr Henschel was quite right, in the face of the flourish of trumpets which heralded Mottl's arrival, to decline to admit the pretensions of the stranger to give us lessons in Wagner conducting; and he could only protest effectively by at once offering a performance by his own band as a sample of what London can do, thus tacitly daring Herr Mottl to beat him.

Nothing could be fairer; nothing could be bolder; nothing could be more entirely creditable to the challenger. If I could add that the invader had been put to shame – that he had done nothing that Mr Henschel had not done as well, or better, then indeed it would be a proud day for London. But to that length I must not go. Mr Henschel, in the heat of his spirit, underrated his adversary. He was not bad; but Mottl bettered him in every bar. Before the Rienzi overture was half through it was evident that London was going to have a most exemplary beating from Carlsruhe. One after another the blemishes and stupidities to which we have become so inured here that we have ceased to record them against our conductors vanished under Mottl's hand.

Let me, before speaking of his highest qualities, give an illustration or two of his resources as a manager of the orchestra. We all know the overture to Tannhäuser by heart by this time. Well, have we not often shrunk from the coarse and unsatisfactory effect of the three trombones at the climax of the pilgrims' march in the first section of the overture? With Richter it is rather worse than with the others, since he insists on the full power of the fortissimo. Mottl effected a magical transformation. The chant was as powerful as Richter could have desired; and yet it was beautiful, broad, easy, with a portamento which an Italian singer might have envied.

How was this brought about? In the simplest way in the world. Instead of keeping strict Procrustean time for the florid work of the violins, thus forcing the trombones to chop their phrases so as to fit the accompaniment, Mottl gave the trombones a free hand, allowing them to give the time to the whole band, and making the violins wait, when necessary between the bars, so to speak, until the slow-speaking brass instruments had turned their phrases with unembarrassed majesty. The effect was magnificent. In exactly the same way and with still more splendid effect, he gave us the great passage at the end of Die Walküre, where the trombones reaffirm the last words of Wotan.

Again, take the Flying Dutchman overture. In the second half of this, the contrast between the furious raging of the storm on the one hand, and the consolation of the salvation theme on the other, should be so obvious, one would think, to any ordinarily imaginative conductor, that Wagner thought it sufficient to indicate the necessary changes of tempo by such hints as ritenuto, stringendo, and the like, depending on their apparent inevitability for their full comprehension. Yet we are accustomed to hear our bands dragged tearing through the salvation theme at almost the same speed as through the storm, some attempt being made to strike a balance by taking the one too slow and the other too fast. Mottl varied his speed from allegro to adagio, managing the transitions with perfect address, and producing the full effect which everybody except our conductors knows to be what Wagner intended.

His allegro, too, was a true *allegro con brio*, as marked, and not the customary *allegro pomposo*. His treatment of those batteries of chords which lead up to the first forte in the quick movement reminded me of Wagner himself, whom I once saw stamping to them with his foot, and, I am afraid, swearing at the band between his teeth because they would not hit them out tremendously enough for him. He would certainly have been satisfied with the cannonade which Mottl got from the drums in this passage. It is one of Mottl's salient characteristics as a conductor that he seizes on the accents of the music with immense energy, always using them to obtain force of expression, and never merely to set people dancing, in the manner of an Austrian band.

This distinction came out strikingly in the instrumental version of Tannhäuser's paean to Venus in the overture, commonly played as if it were something between a march and a galop, under which treatment the two trumpet blasts with which the opening notes are emphasized sound like a rather boyish bit of decoration, as if someone had tipped two out of a row of iron railings with gilding for no particular purpose, except to see the gold glitter. In Mottl's hands these two trumpet notes explained themselves at once as necessary reinforcements of two all-important accents; and the effect was not to make the movement still more march-like, but, on the contrary, to entirely prevent any such suggestion, and to produce the true accent of oratorical passion, the intensive impulses of which are no more like the merely go-ahead lilt of a march or dance than a furnace is like a sky-rocket.

In short, though Mottl is a very forcible conductor, and, in spite of all that has been said about his slowness, a very fast conductor when the right tempo happens to be very fast, he is not in the least an impetuous one: his self-possession is completed instead of destroyed by excitement; and his speed and energy are those of a strong man on level ground, and not those of an ordinary one going downhill. It must not be supposed that this intensive, concentric force, characteristic of the true art passion, is always manifesting itself in the energetic way in him.

For example, his conducting of the Lohengrin prelude was quite a study in physical expression of just the opposite mode of musical feeling. Needless to say, the band fell considerably short of the ethereal perfection of sound at which the composer aimed. Mottl's face and gesture, entreating, imploring, remonstrating, deprecating, pleading, would have softened hearts of stone; and the violins made it as easy for him as they could, which was perhaps not very easy, especially in the first section.

In the Tannhäuser, too, the fine tone and expressive phrasing of the violoncellos at their first entry in the pilgrims' march was something to be for ever grateful for; while the perfect freedom allowed to the clarinet to develop all the sweetness of the Venus strain (which I heard then, for the first time in my life, as it was meant to be heard) produced an effect only surpassed when, at the end of the Tristan prelude, the Liebestod, usually murdered by being taken too fast, came stealing in, with the conductor doing exactly what Wagner declared to be the whole duty of a conductor, 'giving the right time to the band'. Is it vain to hope that nobody will ever take it too fast again?

Perhaps the most convincing instance of Mottl's delicacy of touch was the way in which he managed to veil the cheapness and Rossinian tum-tum of the Rienzi overture, which Mr Henschel had stripped naked with a ruthless hand. But it is unnecessary to multiply illustrations. Those which I have given will serve to shew that I am not merely turning an empty phrase in compliment to a Bayreuth reputation when I say that Mottl is a conductor of the very first rank, with, to boot, immense physical energy and personal influence. I was filled with admiration by his efficiency and insight; and I imagine my feelings were shared by all present who were capable of discriminating between one conductor and another. It is greatly to be desired that Mr Schulz-Curtius should follow up the great success of his enterprise (the room was crammed, and the seats had all been sold months in advance) by establishing an annual series of concerts under Mottl. A second concert is already announced for May 22; but the program will have to be changed in one particular. As it stands at present, Beethoven is represented by the overture to Egmont only. This – with due respect to the authors of the program – is all nonsense. Mottl must conduct the C minor symphony: that is the sample of Beethoven for which all his qualities mark him out. By all means, however, let us have Egmont as well, and sacrifice one of the Wagner selections.

And this brings me to the question of that recent artistic phenomenon, the Wagner program, which, as we are assured by the directors of the Crystal Palace, is the most attractive program nowadays. It may be so; but it is an artistic misdemeanour all the same. In satisfying our craving for the sound of Wagner's music, the concert-room is, against its own nature, doing the work of quite another social organ – to wit, the theatre.

We have, unfortunately, no Wagner theatre here; and we must either leave Wagner unheard, or else stuff our concert programs with selections arranged for orchestra alone, as in the second part of a Covent Garden promenade concert. For an arrangement of the Liebestod for a band is really not a bit more defensible at a first-rate concert than an arrangement of the Miserere scene from Il Trovatore or a Pinafore potpourri. It is better to hear the Bayreuth music done in this way than not to hear it at all, perhaps; but it need not on that account be allowed to squeeze concert music proper out of our concerts. I confess that towards the end of Mr Henschel's program my attention began to wander; and if I had seen Mottl conducting as often as I have seen Mr Henschel, I doubt whether even his concentrated power could hold me with the Parsifal prelude played as postlude to ninety minutes' music.

Indeed, to make the confession complete, I may as well add that my attention to the last piece at the Mottl concert cost me a distinct effort. Something comparatively cheap and violently self-assertive, like the Walkürenritt (which Mottl very properly left out of his scheme) is needed to end long concerts, if long concerts must be inflicted on us. Indeed it would be far more reasonable to take these chronological-order programs backwards, so that we could give our unwearied attention to the best pieces first, and reserve the Rienzi overture to waken us up and demoralize the band when our edge has been well dulled.

I have one other strong reason for desiring to see Mottl established here as a conductor. His greatest rival, Richter, is so far above the heads of the public that he has no external stimulus to do his best in London. Only a very few people can perceive the difference between his best and his second best; but the difference between his second best and Mottl's best would be felt at once by a considerable body of amateurs. Now I do not suggest that Richter ever consciously does less than his best; but I am materialist enough in these matters to believe that even the best man does more work under pressure than in a vacuum. Mr Henschel, for instance, whose concert was not up to his own standard, much less to Mottl's, will be quite able, now that he is put on his mettle, to surpass himself. . . .

Ruskin on Music

➤➤◄◄

2 May 1894

I HAVE been indulging in five shillings' worth of Ruskin on Music, in a volume just published by Mr George Allen. As it happened, the first sentence I lighted on when I opened the book was 'the oratorio, withering the life of religion into dead bones on the Syren sands'. Immediately I woke up; for the fact that modern oratorio is mostly a combination of frivolity and sensuality with hypocrisy and the most oppressive dullness is still sufficiently a trade secret to make its discovery by an outsider interesting. A few pages off I found Mr Ruskin describing the singing he heard south of the Alps. Usually the Englishman in Italy, carefully primed beforehand with literary raptures concerning a nation of born musicians speaking the most vocal language in the world, is sufficiently careful of his own credit as a man of taste to discover a Giuglini in every gondolier and St Cecilia's lute in every accordion.

Mr Ruskin innovated so far to use his own judgment; and here is the result: 'Of bestial howling, and entirely frantic vomiting up of damned souls through their still carnal throats, I have heard more than, please God, I will ever endure the hearing of again, in one of His summers.' I take the liberty of squeezing Mr Ruskin's hand in mute sympathy with the spirit of this passage. In Italy, where the chance of being picked up off the streets and brought out as *primo tenore* at the Opera occupies the

same space in the imagination of the men as the chance of select-
ing a Derby winner does in England, you cannot get away from
the ignoble bawling which Mr Ruskin describes so forcibly – and
yet not too forcibly, or forcibly enough; for language will not
hold the full pretentiousness and cupidity of the thing, let alone
the unpleasantness of the noise it makes.

It is at once the strength and weakness of Mr Ruskin in dealing
with music that he is in love with it. There is always a certain
comedy in the contrast between people as they appear trans-
figured in the eyes of those who love them, and as they appear to
those who are under no such inspiration – or, for the matter of
that, as they appear to themselves. And the tragi-comedy of the
love of men and women for one another is reproduced in their
love for art.

Mr Ruskin is head and ears in love with Music; and so am I;
but I am married to her, so to speak, as a professional critic,
whereas he is still a wooer, and has the illusions of imperfect
knowledge as well as the illuminations of perfect love. Listen to
this, for example:

'True music is the natural expression of a lofty passion for a
right cause. In proportion to the kingliness and force of any
personality, the expression either of its joy or suffering becomes
measured, chastened, calm, and capable of interpretation only
by the majesty of ordered, beautiful, and worded sound. Exactly
in proportion to the degree in which we become narrow in the
cause and conception of our passions, incontinent in the utterance of them, feeble of perseverance in them, sullied or shameful
in the indulgence of them, their expression by musical means
becomes broken, mean, fatuitous, and at last impossible: the
measured waves of heaven will not lend themselves to the expression of ultimate vice: it must be for ever sunk in discordance
or silence.'

I entirely agree with Mr Ruskin in this; but it will not hold
water, for all that. 'The measured waves of heaven' are not so
particular as he thinks. Music will express any emotion, base
or lofty. She is absolutely unmoral: we find her in Verdi's last
work heightening to the utmost the expression of Falstaff's

carnal gloating over a cup of sack, just as willingly as she heightened the expression of 'a lofty passion for a right cause' for Beethoven in the Ninth Symphony. She mocked and prostituted the Orpheus legend for Offenbach just as keenly and effectively as she ennobled it for Gluck. Mr Ruskin himself has given an instance of this – a signally wrong instance, by the way; but let that pass for a moment:

'And yonder musician, who used the greatest power (in the art he knew) the Father of Spirits ever yet breathed into the clay of this world; who used it, I say, to follow and fit with perfect sound the words of the Zauberflöte and of Don Giovanni – foolishest and most monstrous of conceivable human words and subjects of thought – for the future amusement of his race! No such spectacle of unconscious (and in that unconsciousness all the more fearful) moral degradation of the highest faculty to the lowest purpose can be found in history.'

This is a capital instance of Mr Ruskin's besetting sin – virtuous indignation. If these two operas are examples of 'foolishest and most monstrous' words fitted and followed with perfect sound – that is, with true music – what becomes of the definition which limits true music to 'the natural expression of a lofty passion for a right cause'? Clearly, that will not do.

And now may I beg Mr Ruskin to mend his illustration, if not his argument? The generation which could see nothing in Die Zauberflöte but a silly extravaganza was one which Mr Ruskin certainly belonged to in point of time; and he has for once sunk to the average level of its thought in this shallow criticism of the work which Mozart deliberately devoted to the expression of his moral sympathies. Everything that is true and vital in his worship of music would be shattered if it were a fact – happily it is not – that the music of Sarastro came from a silly and trivial mood. If I were to assure Mr Ruskin that Bellini's Madonna with St Ursula, in Venice, was originally knocked off as a sign for a tavern by the painter, Mr Ruskin would simply refuse to entertain the story, no matter what the evidence might be, knowing that the thing was eternally impossible. Since he sees no such impossibility in the case of Die Zauberflöte, I must conclude that he does not know the masterpieces of music as he knows those of painting.

As to Don Giovanni, otherwise The Dissolute One Punished, the only immoral feature of it is its supernatural retributive morality. Gentlemen who break through the ordinary categories of good and evil, and come out at the other side singing Fin ch' han dal vino and La ci darem, do not, as a matter of fact, get called on by statues, and taken straight down through the floor to eternal torments; and to pretend that they do is to shirk the social problem they present. Nor is it yet by any means an established fact that the world owes more to its Don Ottavios than to its Don Juans.

It is, of course, impossible to make a serious stand on a libretto which is such an odd mixture of the old Punch tradition with the highly emancipated modern philosophy of Molière; but whether you apply Mr Ruskin's hasty criticism to Punch and Judy or to Le Festin de Pierre, you will, I think, see that it is fundamentally nothing but an explosion of pious horror of the best Denmark Hill brand. The hard fact is that Don Giovanni is eminent in virtue of its uncommon share of wisdom, beauty, and humor; and if any theory of morals leads to the conclusion that it is foolish and monstrous, so much the worse for the theory.

I must, further, remonstrate with Mr Ruskin about his advice to the girls of England. First, like a veritable serpent in the garden, he tempts the young English lady, already predisposed to self-righteousness, with the following wicked words: 'From the beginning consider all your accomplishments as means of assistance to others.' This is Denmark Hill with a vengeance. But the artist in Mr Ruskin is always getting the better of Denmark Hill; and on the very next page he says, 'Think only of accuracy; never of effect or expression.'

Now, will anyone kindly tell me how a young lady is to consider all her accomplishments 'as means of assistance to others' – that is, to think of nothing but effect and expression, and consequently to cultivate self-consciousness and its attendant personal susceptibility up to the highest point – and at the same time not to think of effect or expression at all, but at only of accuracy. Speaking as a rival sage – as one who, in musical matters at least, considers himself fitted to play Codlin to Mr Ruskin's Short – I earnestly advise the young ladies of England, whether enrolled in the Guild of St George or not, to cultivate music solely for the love and need of it, and to do it in all humility of spirit, never forgetting that they are most likely inflicting all-but-unbearable annoyance on every musician within earshot, instead of rendering 'assistance to others'.

The greatest assistance the average young lady musician can render to others is to stop. Mind, I speak of life as it is. Some day, perhaps, when it is like a page out of Wilhelm Meister or Sesame and Lilies, when the piano is dead and our maidens go up into the mountains to practise their first exercises on the harp, Mr Ruskin's exhortations as to the sinfulness of doing anything merely because you like it may gain some sort of plausibility. At present they will not wash.

'It is, I believe,' says Mr Ruskin, 'as certain that in the last twenty years we have learnt to better understand good music, and to love it more, as that in the same time our knowledge and love of pictures have not increased. The reason is easily found. Our music has been chosen for us by masters; and our pictures have been chosen by ourselves.'

Alas! how easy it is to find a reason for the thing that is not! Not that there is not here, as usual, a hundred times more insight in Mr Ruskin's mistake than in most other men's accuracies. It is quite true that the favorite works at our good concerts are of a much higher class than the favorite works at the Royal Academy, and that the difference is due to the fact that Beethoven and Wagner are still in a position to dictate to the public what is good for them. But the public is not really conscious of that part of Beethoven's work which raises it above the level of popular painting. It finds a great deal of Beethoven incomprehensible, and therefore dull, putting up with it only because the alternative is either no music at all or something a good deal duller. But will it put up with it when vulgar musicians have completely mastered the trade of producing symphonies and operas containing all the cheap, popular, obvious, carnal luxuries of the Beethovenian music, without its troublesome nobilities, depths, and spiritual grandeurs?

I doubt it. Wagner accused Meyerbeer of following the great masters as a starling follows the plough, picking up the titbits which their force unearthed, and serving them up to Paris unmixed with nobler matter. That process, which has been going on in music for less than a century, has been going on in painting for three or four hundred years, so that our contemporary popular painters have rid themselves far more completely of what was greatest in the great masters of Florence, Rome, and Venice, than our contemporary composers of what was greatest in Mozart, Beethoven, and Wagner; but the process is going on all the same under the influence of popular demand; and we shall soon have the field held by vulgar music as much as by vulgar painting, as is right and proper in a country with a vulgar population.

I need hardly add that Mr Ruskin himself, true to his method of never collating his utterances, but taking his inspiration as it comes, so that on every possible subject he says the right thing and the wrong thing with equal eloquence within the same ten minutes, does not really believe any such nonsense as that people can be kept on high ground by having their music chosen for them by masters. For instance:

'You cannot paint or sing yourselves into being good men. You must be good men before you can either paint or sing; and then the color and the sound will complete all in you that is best.'

Neither can people appreciate good music, whether chosen for them by masters or not, except to the extent to which they are 'good' themselves. You can chain a terrier to Richter's desk, and force it to listen to all the symphonies of Beethoven, without changing its opinion one jot as to the relative delights of rat-hunting and classical music; and the same thing is true in its degree of mankind. The real point is, that most of us, far from being chained to the desk, never get the chance of finding out whether we can appreciate great music or not.

Mr Ruskin is probably right in anticipating that a change in the tone of public feeling would be produced 'if, having been accustomed only to hear black Christy's, blind fiddlers, and hoarse beggars scrape and howl about their streets, the people were permitted daily audience of faithful and gentle orchestral rendering of the work of the highest classical masters.'

Here I must leave an infinitely suggestive and provocative book, the publication of which no musical critic can very well ignore. To finish, I will give, without comment, one more quotation as a sample of what Mr Ruskin's musical criticism would, perhaps, have been like if he had taken to my branch of the trade instead of to his own:

'Grisi and Malibran sang at least one-third slower than any modern cantatrice; and Patti, the last time I heard her, massacred Zerlina's part in La ci darem, as if the audience and she had but the one object of getting Mozart's air done with as soon as possible. . . . Afterwards I was brought to the point of trying to learn to sing, in which, though never even getting so far as to read with ease, I nevertheless, between my fine rhythmic ear and true-lover's sentiment, got to understand some principles of musical art, which I shall perhaps be able to enforce, with benefit on the musical public mind, even today.'

Patti

⇥⭤⭩

30 May 1894

WE live in an age of progress. Patti has been singing a song by Wagner. Never shall I forget the sensation among the critics at the Albert Hall when, on turning over the pages of their programs, they saw among the names there that of The Master, cropping up like a modest crocus among those of Mozart, Rossini, and other contemporaries of Madame Patti's grandmother. There is now no denying the fact that Madame Patti – Adelina Patti – *the* Patti – the lady who used to appear and reappear as Rosina in Il Barbiere at Covent Garden until the old régime died of it, actually did, on the afternoon of Saturday, May 19, 1894, sing the study on Tristan und Isolde, No 5 of the Five Poems composed by Richard Wagner, late of Bayreuth, in 1862. What is more, she sang it extremely well, and, when the inevitable encore came, repeated it instead of singing Home, Sweet Home or Within a Mile.

And yet there was something exasperating in the thought that this demonstration by a fine singer that Wagner's music is as singable as Mozart's came just twenty years after it was most needed. Nobody now supposes that in Wagner's works the women must shriek and the men howl, and that no human voice can stand the wear and tear for more than a year or two. But that was once a very common opinion, most devoutly acted on by many operatic artists, with, of course, fully corroborative results as far as the prophesied wear and tear was concerned. What was Madame Patti doing in those dark days, when she might have rescued Tannhäuser from the horrors of its first performance at Covent Garden in the decline and fall of the seventies? Alas! in those days she sang Bel raggio in the key of A, and did not sing Wagner at all.

It was left to Jean de Reszke, by his Walther in Die Meistersinger, to give the final proof that Wagner requires and repays the most delicate lyrical treatment; and now Madame Patti, with the ground made safe for her, comes forward and, having first propitiated the first quarter of the expiring century by singing Bel raggio in the key of G, at last ventures on this simple little Träume, and is perhaps surprised to find that the thrill is deeper and the applause more sincere than that which follows Rossini's shallow bravura. For my part, I regard Patti's brilliancy as a singer of florid decorative music as one of her greatest misfortunes. In the first place, she has never done it superlatively well: it has always been a little jerky and tricky in comparison with the finest execution of such a perfect singer of roulade as Marimon, for instance, not to mention others.

I never fully appreciated Patti until one night at Covent Garden when I heard her sing, not Una Voce or anything of that sort, but God save the Queen. The wonderful even soundness of the middle of her voice, its beauty and delicacy of surface, and her exquisite touch and diction, all qualify her to be great in expressive melody, and to occupy a position in the republic of art high above the pretty flummery of newspaper puffs, flowers, recalls, encores, and so forth which makes it so difficult for people who take art seriously to do justice to the talent and the artistic pains with which she condescends to bid for such recognition.

I am so far from regretting that Time has stolen some of the five or six notes above the high B flat which she once possessed, and has made the rest hardly safe for everyday use, that I shall heartily congratulate her when the day comes when Bel raggio and Ah, non giunge, in any key whatsoever, must be dropped, and replaced in her repertory by more such songs as Träume; for it is my firm belief that Patti is capable of becoming a great singer, though the world has been at such pains and expense to spoil her for the last thirty-five years. At her concert on the 19th, her voice was better than at last year's concerts; and altogether she was brighter, more efficient, more successful – if there can be said to be degrees in Patti's success – than when I last heard her....

Stanford on the Critics

→–◄–◄

13 June 1894

Dr Villiers Stanford has been favoring us with his views on Some Aspects of Musical Criticism in England in the shape of a magazine article. I am very strongly tempted to quote it here at full length; for it is the best article I ever saw on the subject, unexceptionally judicious and accurate, and much better written than most musical criticisms are. I shall at least quote his exposition of his main point, as I cannot paraphrase it to any advantage:

'A new opera, which has been, perhaps, the work of years, and the outcome of the daily thought and labor of composer and librettist, is produced on a Monday night; and by 2 a.m. on Tuesday morning a critic, who has just made his first acquaintance with the composition, is expected to have completed a full and just chronicle of its merits and faults, its workmanship and its effect, fit to be put into print, and intended to instruct the public before breakfast as to what attitude they should be prepared to take when they find themselves in the audience. I say, as one who is, from much experience in the musician's craft, perhaps exceptionally quick in seizing the points of a new work at first hearing, that to expect the best possible criticism, or indeed criticism of any lasting value at all under such circumstances is grotesque; and the insistence upon such hot haste production is a hardship to the writer, an injury to the producer, and a mischief to the public.'

True as this is, and deeply as I am touched by the tribute here implied, and elsewhere explicitly rendered, to the superiority of those weekly articles of which my own may be taken as examples, I am not sure that the opinion elaborated in a week is always so much more valuable than the impression made in a moment. The only musical compositions which will bear thinking of for more than half an hour are those which require an intimate acquaintance of at least ten years for their critical mastery. As to the weekly article being any more 'just' than the daily one, I do not see how that can be sustained for a moment. Let us try to vivify our ideas on the subject by getting away from the abstraction 'criticism' to the reality from which it is abstracted : that is, the living, breathing, erring, human, nameable and addressable individual who writes criticism.

To avoid getting into trouble I shall not cite any musical critics. The dramatic and parliamentary ones will serve my turn as well. Two of the best dramatic critics in London, Mr Clement Scott and Mr Walkley, write both weekly essays and two-o'clock-in-the-morning notices of new plays. Both write the immediate notice as impressionists. Mr Scott writes his deferred notice also as an impressionist, rubbing in his first impression, and as often as not spoiling it. Mr Walkley is an acute analyst; and in his case the gain in intellectual elaboration in the deferred notice is immense. But has anyone ever observed any gain in either case in the matter of justice? I certainly never have.

Take another case in point. I have for years urged upon editors the necessity of sending a fine critic into the House of Commons to write notices of the sittings of the House exactly as they send a critic to the Opera. The result of giving such a critic a brief for Lord Rosebery against Lord Salisbury is as absurd as it would be to give me a brief for Calvé as against Melba, or my colleague W. A. a brief for Mr Irving as against Mr Tree. Of late years the custom of prefacing the verbatim reports of the sittings of the House by a descriptive report has been developing parliamentary criticism on my lines.

For example, Mr Massingham, a typical parliamentary critic of the new kind, will, in criticizing a debate, praise the performances of Mr Balfour and Mr John Burns, and slate Sir William Harcourt and Mr Chamberlain, or vice versa, as if there were no such thing as party politics in the world. This sounds impartial; but does anybody find Mr Massingham 'just'; or is it likely that he would be any the juster if his extraordinary small-hour performances were replaced by weekly ones? The fact is, justice is not the critic's business; and there is no more dishonest and insufferable affectation in criticism than that impersonal, abstract, judicially authoritative air which, since it is so easy to assume, and so well adapted to rapid phrase stringing, is directly encouraged by the haste which Dr Stanford deprecates.

In Dr Stanford's article, which is a masterpiece in the way of tact, no individual critic now alive and working on the English press is talked either of or at. Instead, we have 'the critic', 'the musical correspondent', and so on. Now 'the critic' is a very fine character. One can quite believe that if only the noble creature is given time to consider his utterances, he will hold the scales balanced to a hair's breadth. But just substitute for 'the critic' the initials G.B.S. Instantly the realities of the case leap to light; and you see without any argument that the lapse of a few days between the performance and the notice, far from obliterating the writer's partialities and prejudices, his personal likes and dislikes, his bias, his temperament, his local traditions, his nationality – in a word, himself, only enables him to express them the more insidiously when he wishes to conceal their influence.

No man sensitive enough to be worth his salt as a critic could for years wield a pen which, from the nature of his occupation, is scratching somebody's nerves at every stroke, without becoming conscious of how monstrously indefensible the superhuman attitude of impartiality is for him. If the countless injustices which I have done in these columns had been perpetuated in that attitude I should deserve hanging. I therefore add to Dr Stanford's plea for the more considerate utterance of the weekly feuilleton, a further plea for sincerity of expression, not only of the critic's opinion, but of the mood in which that opinion was formed.

We cannot get away from the critic's tempers, his impatiences, his sorenesses, his friendships, his spite, his enthusiasms (amatory and other), nay, his very politics and religion if they are touched by what he criticizes. They are all there hard at work; and it should be his point of honor – as it is certainly his interest if he wishes to avoid being dull – not to attempt to conceal them or to offer their product as the dispassionate dictum of infallible omniscience. If the public were to receive such a self exhibition by coldly saying, 'We dont want to know the sort of person you are : we want to know whether such a work or artist or performance is good or bad,' then the critic could unanswerably retort, 'How on earth can you tell how much my opinion on that point is worth unless you know the sort of person I am?' As a matter of fact the public never does meet a good critic with any such rebuff. The critic who cannot interest the public in his real self has mistaken his trade : that is all.

Dr Stanford touches a painful point when he speaks of 'the danger that editors who happen themselves to be ignorant of music, should engage the services of writers almost equally ignorant merely because they possess the gift of literary style.' Here, for almost the only moment in his article, Dr Stanford speaks without inside knowledge of journalism. Editors, by some law of Nature which still baffles science, are *always* ignorant of music, and consequently always abjectly superstitious on the subject. Instead of looking the more keenly to the critic's other qualifications because they cannot judge of his musical ones, they regard him with an awe which makes them incapable of exercising any judgment at all about him.

Find me an editor who can tell at a glance whether a review, a leading article, a London letter, or a news paragraph is the work of a skilled hand or not, and who has even some power of recognizing what is money's worth and what is not in the way of a criticism of the Royal Academy or the last new play; and I, by simply writing that 'the second subject, a graceful and flowing theme contrasting happily with the rugged vigor of its predecessor, appears unexpectedly in the key of the dominant,' will reduce that able editor to a condition so abject that he will let me inundate his columns with pompous platitude, with the dullest plagiarisms from analytic programs, with shameless puffery, with bad grammar, bad logic, wrong dates, wrong names, with every conceivable blunder and misdemeanor that a journalist can commit, provided I do it in the capacity of his musical critic.

Not that my stuff will not bore and worry him as much as it will bore and worry other people; but what with his reluctance to risk a dispute with me on a subject he does not understand, and his habit of considering music as a department of lunacy, practised and read about by people who are not normally sane and healthy human beings, he will find it easiest to 'suppose it is all right' and to console himself with the reflection that it does not matter anyhow. Dr Stanford says, 'If editors appoint an incompetent person, public opinion is pretty sure, sooner or later, to find out and expose the ignoramus.' This expectation is so entirely and desperately unwarranted by experience, that I may take it that Dr Stanford only offers it rather than leave the difficulty without at least a pretence of a solution.

But why not form a Vigilance Committee of musicians for the exposure of incompetent critics? The other day, as we all remember, five eminent musicians published a protest against a certain musical critic. Being new to their work, they did not do it well; and the critic got the best of it; but I sincerely hope the five will not be discouraged. After a few trials, a Vigilance Committee would learn to attack cautiously and effectively, and to avoid the professional weakness of exaggerating the importance of those blunders as to historic facts and musical technicalities which sometimes give a ludicrous air to really shrewd and essentially sound criticism.

Musical criticisms, like sermons, are of low average quality simply because they are never discussed or contradicted; and I should rejoice were such a committee to be formed, especially if Dr Stanford were to be chairman, and would undertake the drafting of such public protests as it might be deemed advisable to issue. . . .